OXFO[

Picture Power Dictionary

1500 words through stories and pictures

Stories by Stella Maidment

Illustrated by Belinda Evans

GLOBAL VILLAG
SP. Z O.O.
Al. Legionów 42, 25-035 Kielce
tel. (41) 345-43-68, tel/fax 362-10-20
e-mail global@complex.com.p
NIP 657-031-18-52 Reg. 29035095€

Oxford University Press

Oxford University Press, Great Clarendon Street, Oxford OX2 6DP

Oxford New York
Athens Auckland Bangkok Bogota Bombay Buenos Aires
Calcutta Cape Town Dar es Salaam Delhi Florence Hong Kong
Istanbul Karachi Kuala Lumpur Madras Madrid Melbourne
Mexico City Nairobi Paris Singapore Taipei Tokyo Toronto Warsaw

and associated companies in
Berlin Ibadan

OXFORD and OXFORD ENGLISH
are trade marks of Oxford University Press

ISBN 0 19 431420 0
© Oxford University Press 1996

First published 1996
Second impression 1997

Acknowledgements

Stories by Stella Maidment
Illustrated by Belinda Evans
Maps by Hardlines, Charlbury, Oxon
Entertainments guide by Tim Slade
Designed by Richard Morris, Stonesfield Design
Printed in Hong Kong

How to use this book

This book may be used in class or at home to teach basic English
vocabulary to children. The Oxford Picture Power Dictionary
Cassette (ISBN 0 19 431436 7) contains a reading of the stories
and words in the dictionary. Oxford Picture Power Activity Book
(ISBN 0 19 431446 4) provides a wide range of activities to
practise the vocabulary of the dictionary.

Contents

1   our family

Jill is looking at photographs of her family.

Jill I have one brother, two parents, four grandparents, three aunts, two uncles, and four cousins. My brother's called Mike. We call our parents Mum and Dad.

Mum has a sister called Jenny and a brother called Paul. Uncle Paul is married to Sarah.

Their baby, Lucy, is my cousin. Mum's mother and father are my grandmother and grandfather. I call them Granny and Grandad.

Dad has one sister, my Auntie Helen. Auntie Helen and Uncle Tim have three children, Ben, Tom, and Becky. They are my cousins. I call Dad's parents Grandma and Grandpa. There are lots of names for children to call their grandparents.

grandmother   grandfather   grandmother   grandfather

grandparents

Granny   Grandad   parents   Grandma   Grandpa

aunt   uncle   aunt   mother   father   aunt   uncle

Auntie Sarah   Uncle Paul   Auntie Jenny   Mum   Dad   Auntie Helen   Uncle Tim

cousin   brother   me   cousin   cousin   cousin

Lucy   Mike   Jill   Ben   Tom   Becky

Mike Write a, b, c, or d by the right photo.

a That's Ben in his black jacket and Uncle Tim with his red beard and blue coat. I'm cleaning Becky's glasses with my scarf.

b Here's Granny and Grandad with baby Lucy. Granny made Lucy's yellow hat and cardigan but they're too big. Lucy likes Grandad's moustache.

Grandad is wearing his grey suit and Granny is wearing her purple dress.

c That's Tom in his green sweater and shorts and me in my white T-shirt and jeans. There's Becky in her red sweatshirt and leggings. One of her boots is falling off.

d I don't know who took this photo. I can see my trainers and jeans, my sister's orange dress, Mum's pink skirt and red sandals, and Dad's brown trousers and shoes. I think it's a photo of me, Jill, Mum, and Dad.

1 moustache	5 hat	9 T-shirt	13 glove	17 scarf	21 skirt
2 shirt	6 dress	10 sweatshirt	14 jacket	18 coat	22 trainer
3 suit	7 shorts	11 leggings	15 glasses	19 jeans	23 shoe
4 cardigan	8 sweater	12 boot	16 beard	20 trousers	24 sandal

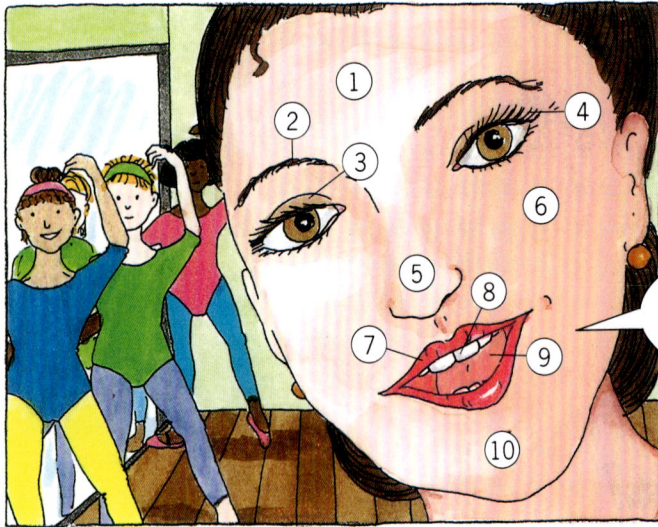

Miss Gwen's face

Jill likes dancing. Her teacher is called Miss Gwen.

Head up!
Stomach in! Good!

1 forehead	4 eyelash
2 eyebrow	5 nose
3 eyelid	6 cheek
	7 lip
	8 tooth
	9 tongue
	10 chin

head
back
arm
wrist
bottom
leg

hair
mouth
neck
hip

eye
ear
shoulder
elbow
chest
stomach
knee
ankle
toe

hand
finger
thumb

foot   heel

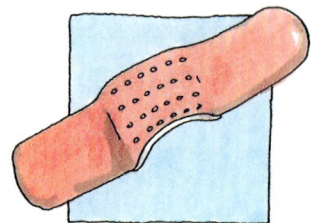

plaster

medicine

Jill hurt her ankle at the dancing class. Now she's waiting to see the doctor. There are other patients waiting too. There is a man with a bad cold and a woman with a headache. One of the woman's sons has a black eye and a bruise on his knee. The other son has toothache and a big plaster on his leg. The doctor is giving a baby an injection.

Now Jill and her mother see the doctor.

Doctor Hello, Jill. What's the matter?

Jill I've hurt my ankle.

Doctor Yes ... you've got some cuts and bruises, Jill, but your ankle isn't broken. I'll put a bandage on it for you.

Jill Thank you, doctor.

headache

toothache

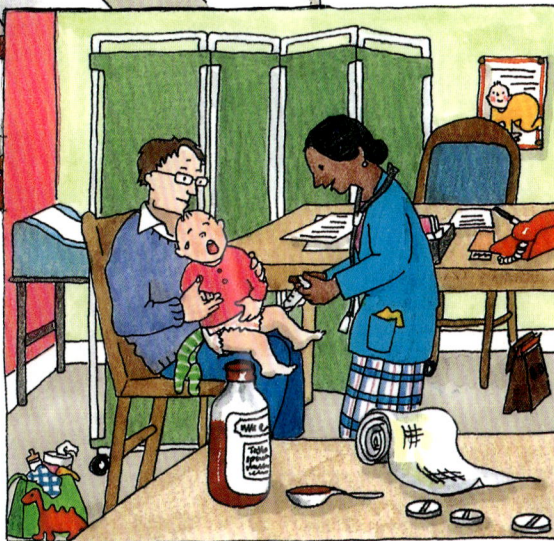

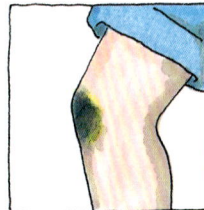

bruise

black eye

cold

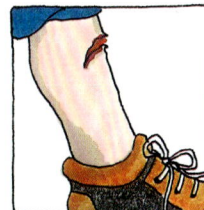

cut

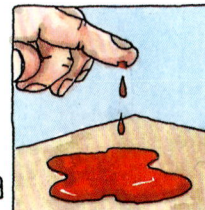

blood

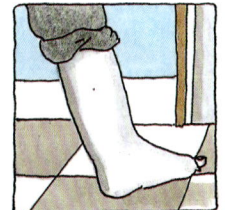

broken leg

pill

bandage

injection

doctor

patient

nurse

5   the house

This is Jill and Mike's house. They live here with Mum and Dad, Muddy the dog, and two cats, Tabby and Leo. It's a big house. There's a wall round the garden and a white gate.

Jill is in the living room. There's a mirror over the fireplace and flowers in a vase. Jill is sitting in an armchair. The lamp is on and she is reading. Muddy is on the rug by the fire. He likes sitting on the sofa but he makes the cushions dirty.

Mike is in the dining room. He's sitting on a chair at the table. The door is open. Tabby is in the hall and Leo is on the stairs.

What's that noise? Is it Mum in the garage? No, it's Dad singing in the bath! The window is open but Dad isn't cold because the water is hot. The bath, the washbasin, and the toilet are blue. The curtains, the carpet, the towels, the toothpaste, and the toothbrushes are blue too. Everything in the bathroom is blue except Dad!

wall   gate   stairs

door   window

fire   fireplace   lamp

table   chair   armchair   sofa

garage

mirror   vase   carpet   rug   cushion   curtain

aerial

chimney

roof

bathroom

hall

bedroom

living room

dining room

bath

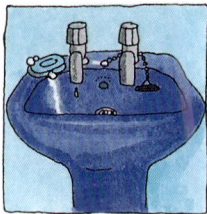

washbasin

toilet

towel

toothpaste

toothbrush

Mike and Jill are helping in the kitchen. Jill is putting the plates and the glasses in the dishwasher. She's putting the knives, forks, and spoons in the dishwasher too. The saucepans and the frying pan are by the sink.

Dad is filling the kettle with water from the tap. He's making some tea. Mum likes her tea in a cup and saucer but Dad likes his tea in a mug. Mum's getting a jug from the fridge. The fridge and the freezer are by the washing machine.

16.00

teatime

Mike is putting the salt and pepper in the cupboard. Oh, there's a bowl for the dishwasher! Jill and Mike made a cake today and it's in the oven now. Mike looks at the clock. It's nearly teatime!

teapot

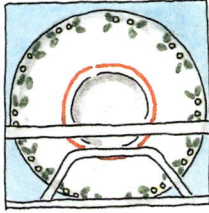
plate

cup

saucer

jug

mug

glass

bowl

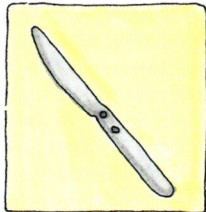
knife

fork

spoon

frying pan

saucepan

salt

pepper

kettle

tap

sink

washing
machine

dishwasher

clock

oven

cake

fridge

freezer

cupboard

This is Jill's room. Jill is putting a poster on the wall above her bed and Leo is sitting on the bed next to Jill's teddy bear. Jill's slippers are by the bed, her pyjamas are under the bed, and her dressing gown is behind the door.

Jill isn't wearing socks. Where are her socks? There's a purple sock between the clock and the lamp and there's a yellow sock round the plant. There's another purple sock in the drawer.

Jill's school photo is at the top of her noticeboard. There's a postcard from Jill's friend in London below the photo. Jill's key is in the middle of the noticeboard.

There's a computer on Jill's desk. Tabby is sitting in front of the computer.

We're going now. Where are your shoes and socks?

at the top

in the middle

at the bottom

on

under

round

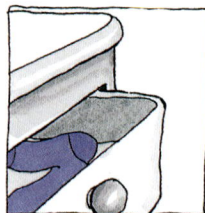

in

above

below

next to

between

by

behind

My shoes are at the bottom of the wardrobe but I can't find my socks!

1 poster	4 plant	16 teddy bear
2 clothes	5 shoe	17 bed
3 dressing gown	6 wardrobe	18 postcard
	7 sock	19 key
	8 brush	20 noticeboard
	9 comb	21 pyjamas
10 chest of drawers		22 slipper
		23 ruler
11 drawer		24 rubber
12 tights		25 computer
13 vest		26 pencil
14 pants		27 calculator
15 toys		28 desk
		29 pen
		30 watch

in front of

11   Jill's week

12.00 It's twelve o'clock. It's midday.

24.00 It's twelve o'clock. It's midnight.

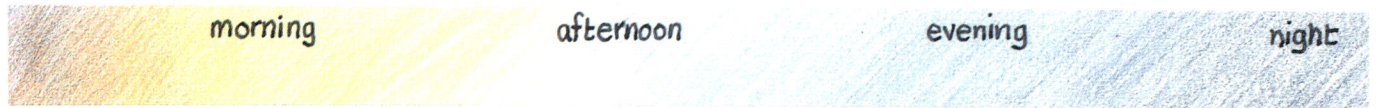

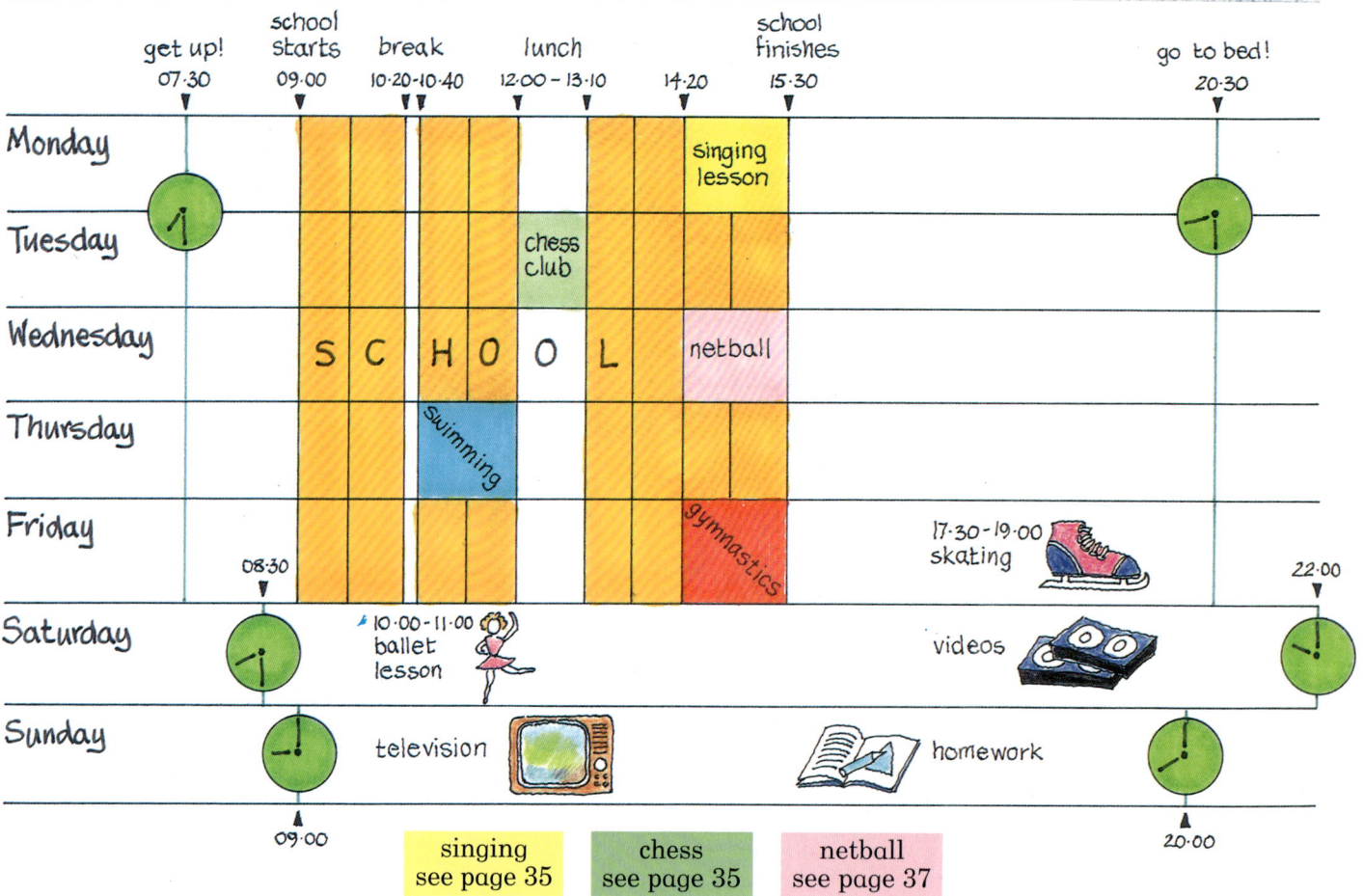

| | morning | | | afternoon | | | evening | | night |

	get up! 07.30	school starts 09.00	break 10.20-10.40	lunch 12.00 – 13.10	14.20	school finishes 15.30			go to bed! 20.30
Monday						singing lesson			
Tuesday				chess club					
Wednesday		S C H O O L				netball			
Thursday			swimming						
Friday	08.30					gymnastics	17.30 – 19.00 skating		22.00
Saturday		10.00 – 11.00 ballet lesson					videos		
Sunday		television					homework		20.00

09.00

| singing
see page 35 | chess
see page 35 | netball
see page 37 |

On weekdays Jill gets up at half past seven. She has a shower, gets dressed, and brushes her hair. Jill has breakfast at eight o'clock and leaves home at half past eight. She goes to school by car.

School starts at nine o'clock. Break is from twenty past ten until twenty to eleven. Jill goes outside at break. On Thursday mornings Jill goes swimming. She has lunch at school at midday. On Tuesdays Jill goes to chess club in her lunch break.

On Monday afternoons Jill has a singing lesson and on Wednesdays she plays netball. On Friday afternoons she does gymnastics. Jill likes Fridays best. School finishes at half past three. Jill and Mike catch the bus home.

On Friday evenings Jill goes skating. Jill's family have dinner at about seven o'clock. On weekdays Jill goes to bed at half past eight. On Saturdays she has a ballet lesson in the morning and watches videos with her friends in the evening. Jill goes to bed late on Saturday nights but on Sunday nights she does her homework and goes to bed early.

o'clock

five to | five past

ten to | ten past

a quarter to | a quarter past

twenty to | twenty past

twenty-five to | twenty-five past

half past

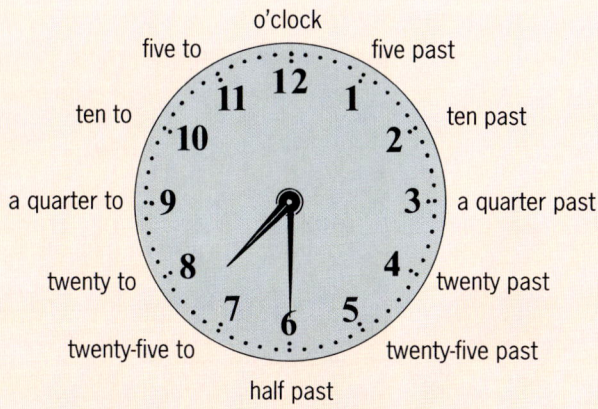

07.30 It's half past seven.

at 07.30 — She gets up.

at 07.35 — She has a shower.

at 07.45 — She gets dressed.

at 07.55 — She brushes her hair.

at 08.00 — She has breakfast.

at 08.30 — She leaves home.

She goes to school by car.

at 10.20 — She goes outside at break.

at 10.40 on Thursdays — She goes swimming.

at 12.00 — She has lunch.

at 14.20 on Fridays — She does gymnastics.

at 15.30 — She catches a bus home.

at 17.30 on Fridays — She goes skating.

at 10.00 on Saturdays — She has a ballet lesson.

on Saturday evenings — She watches videos.

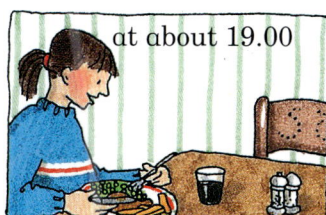

at about 19.00 — She has dinner.

on Sunday evenings — She does her homework.

at 20.30 on weekdays — She goes to bed.

a busy Sunday

She is washing up.

She is cooking.

He is ironing.

He is tidying his room.

He is sweeping the path.

She is cutting the hedge.

He is pushing a wheelbarrow.

They are mending the fence.

He is hammering.

She is washing her dog.

She is pulling Muddy.

He is barking.

He is digging.

Jill and Mike are at their cousins' house. Grandma and Grandpa are there too and everybody is working.

Mum, Grandma, and Ben are downstairs in the kitchen. Mum is washing up, Grandma is cooking, and Ben is ironing. Tom is upstairs. He is tidying his room.

In the garden Uncle Tim is sweeping the path. Auntie Helen is cutting the hedge and Mike is pushing a wheelbarrow. Grandpa and Dad are mending the fence. Dad is hammering loudly!

Becky is washing her dog, Snowy. Jill is pulling Muddy into the water. Muddy is barking. He doesn't like baths.

In the next garden Mr Walker is digging and Mrs Walker is cleaning her car. Kate Walker is feeding the birds. The birds are looking at Kate - and Kate's cat is looking at the birds.

Someone is knocking at the door. It's Tom's friend, Joe. 'Come in!' says Mum. 'There's lots of work to do!'

He is knocking at the door.

She is cleaning her car.

She is feeding the birds.

The cat is looking at the birds.

They are carrying some books.

He is picking up a book.

She is lying down.

She is smiling.

He is laughing.

She is crying.

He is shouting.

He is skipping.

He is standing.

He is walking.

He is running.

She is throwing a ball.

She is hitting a ball.

She is catching a ball.

He is kicking a ball.

She is chasing them.

He is falling over.

She is swinging on a rope.

They are fighting.

She is sitting.

She is hiding.

He is jumping.

He is clapping.

He is climbing.

She is falling.

counter　　dice　　square

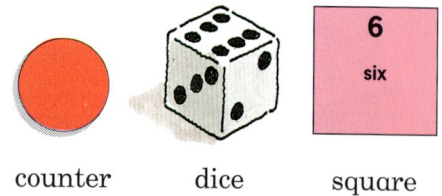

1 Jill and Mike are playing a game.

2 They put their counters on START.

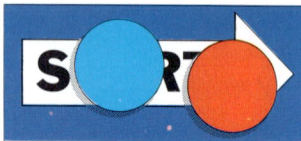

3 Jill throws the dice.

4 She moves to square six.

5 Mike throws the dice.

6 He moves to square five.

7 Can he answer the question?

Five times three is fifteen.

START ↓	↓ **33** What is **thirty-three** times two?	**32** thirty-two	**31** → What is **thirty-one** minus twenty-five?	**30** thirty	**29** twenty-nine
	↑ **34** What is **thirty-four** divided by two?	**63** sixty-three	← **62** What is **sixty-two** plus thirteen?	**61** sixty-one	**60** sixty
1 one	↓ **35** What is **thirty-five** plus sixteen?	**64** sixty-four	↓ **85** What is **eighty-five** plus nine?	**84** → What is **eighty-four** divided by four?	**83** eighty-three
↓ **2** What is **two** times eight?	**36** thirty-six	↓ **65** What is **sixty-five** plus fifteen?	↓ **86** What is **eighty-six** plus eleven?	**99** ninety-nine	**98** → What is **ninety-eight** minus fifty-eight?
3 three	**37** thirty-seven	**66** sixty-six	**87** eighty-seven	**100** one hundred	**F**
↓ **4** four	↑ **38** What is **thirty-eight** minus sixteen?	**67** sixty-seven	**88** eighty-eight	**89** eighty-nine	**90** What is **ninety** plus ten?
↓ **5** What is **five** times three?	**39** thirty-nine	**68** sixty-eight	**69** sixty-nine	← **70** What is **seventy** minus eighteen?	**71** seventy-one
6 six	**40** forty	**41** → What is **forty-one** plus twelve?	← **42** What is **forty-two** divided by seven?	**43** forty-three	**44** forty-four
	7 → What is **seven** times three?	**8** eight	← **9** What is **nine** divided by three?	**10** → What is **ten** times three?	**11** What is **eleven** times two?

× ÷ − +
times divided by minus plus

28 twenty-eight	27 twenty-seven	26 twenty-six	25 → What is **twenty-five** minus eight?	24 → What is **twenty-four** divided by eight?	●
59 fifty-nine	58 fifty-eight	57 fifty-seven	56 fifty-six	55 fifty-five	↑ 23 What is **twenty-three** plus sixteen?
82 eighty-two	81 eighty-one	80 eighty	79 seventy-nine	↓ 54 What is **fifty-four** minus fourteen?	22 twenty-two
97 ninety-seven	96 → What is **ninety-six** divided by twelve?	95 ninety-five	78 seventy-eight	53 fifty-three	21 twenty-one
NISH	94 ninety-four		↓ 77 What is **seventy-seven** minus nine?	52 fifty-two	↓ 20 What is **twenty** minus twelve?
91 ninety-one	92 ninety-two	← 93 What is **ninety-three** minus thirteen	↓ 76 What is **seventy-six** minus sixteen?	51 fifty-one	↑ 19 What is **nineteen** plus thirteen?
← 72 What is **seventy-two** divided by twelve?	73 seventy-three	74 seventy-four	75 seventy-five	↓ 50 What is **fifty** minus fourteen?	↑ 18 What is **eighteen** times two?
← 45 What is **forty-five** divided by fifteen?	46 forty-six	47 forty-seven	48 forty-eight	49 forty-nine	17 seventeen
← 12 What is **twelve** divided by three?	13 → What is **thirteen** times two?	14 → What is **fourteen** times two?	15 fifteen	16 sixteen	●

8 He moves to square fifteen.

15

9 Now it's Jill's turn. She throws the dice.

10 She moves to square twelve.

← 12

11 Can she answer the question?

> Twelve divided by three is four.

12 Jill moves back to square four.

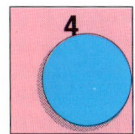

4

13 ... Mike finishes the game in ten minutes. He moves to square one hundred. Mike wins.

NISH

> Can you finish in ten minutes?

paint

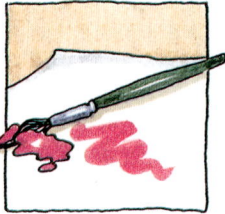
paintbrush

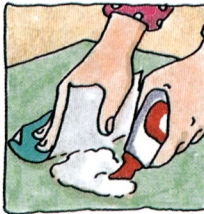
glue

scissors

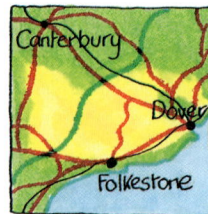
map

lunch box

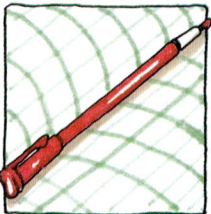
pen

pencil

pencil
sharpener

rubber

ruler

compasses

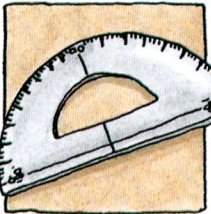
protractor

calculator

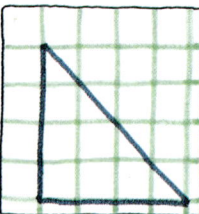
triangle

rectangle

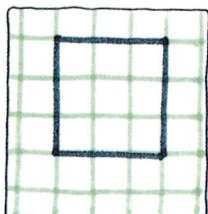
square

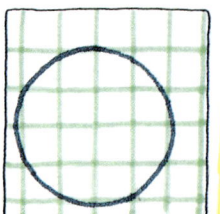
circle

This is Mike's classroom. He is ten years old and he is in Year 6. Jill is nine years old and she is in Year 5. There's a plan of the school on the wall. It's a big school. It has lots of classrooms, a hall, a library, a computer room, a music room, a gym, a science lab, and a sports field.

Mike is having a maths lesson. His teacher is writing on the blackboard and Mike is writing in his exercise book. Mike doesn't like maths.

Mike is hungry. His lunch box is on the shelf in the classroom. He looks at the ceiling, then he looks at the floor. He is thinking about his lunch.

'What's the answer, Mike?' says his teacher. Oh dear, Mike doesn't like maths!

1 boy

6 exercise book

7 textbook

10 bin

15 blackboard

2 girl

11 desk

16 chalk

3 picture

8 paper

12 bookcase

17 ceiling

4 shelf

9 floor

13 globe

18 wall

5 pencil case

14 teacher

classroom

hall

library

computer room

staffroom

music room

gym

science lab

sports field

market

butcher

hairdresser

chemist

flat

newsagent

Jill and Mike are looking for their mother. They know she's in town, but where is she?

They look in the market. She's not there.

They cross the road and look in the shops. They look in the butcher's, the hairdresser's, and the chemist's. They don't see Mum. A woman is standing at the bus stop. It isn't Mum.

Mrs Jenkins lives in a flat above the chemist's. She sees Mike and Jill.

'Hello! What are you doing?'

'We're looking for Mum.'

'Oh yes, I saw her talking to a man with a pushchair.'

They go round the corner. They see John talking to a police officer and Emma coming out of the newsagent's with her mother. They go past the baker's to the post office. There's a woman with a pram by the postbox. She's talking to a man with a pushchair. It's Uncle Paul.

'Hello!' says Uncle Paul. 'Are you looking for your mother? She went to the bank.'

They go to the crossing by the supermarket. The traffic lights change to red, the cars stop, and they go across the road to the bank. Is that Mum in the telephone box on the corner? No, it's a man!

Then Jill says 'Look! There's Muddy sitting on the pavement by the lamp-post. And there's Mum sitting in the café!'

road

pavement

corner

police officer

bus stop

baker

post office

postbox

supermarket

bank

café

pushchair

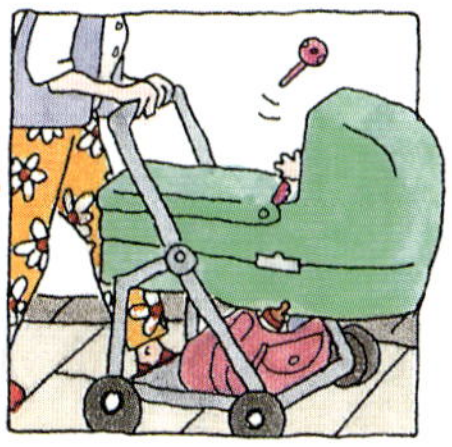

pram

traffic lights

crossing

telephone box

lamp-post

23 in the market

Jill, Mike, and Mum are in the market. Mum is buying vegetables from Mr Perkins and Mike is buying fruit from Mrs Perkins. Jill is reading Mum's shopping list.

Mr Perkins Hello. Can I help you?
Mum Have you got the list, Jill?
Jill Yes. We need potatoes.
Mum Oh yes, three pounds of potatoes, please.
Jill And tomatoes.
Mum And a pound of tomatoes.
Jill And a lettuce.
Mum And a lettuce ... a big one please.
Jill And a cucumber.
Mum How much are the cucumbers?
Mr Perkins They're eighty pence each.
Mum I'll have two, please.
Mr Perkins Anything else?
Mum Is there anything else, Jill?
Jill No.
Mum No, that's all, thank you.
Mr Perkins That's four pounds sixty pence, please.
Mum There's five pounds. Thank you.
Mr Perkins And there's forty pence change. Thank you. Goodbye.

one penny/
one pence

two pence

five pence

one pound

```
          PERKINS
potatoes (£0.25/lb)    3lb    £0.75
tomatoes (£1.60/lb)    1lb    £1.60
lettuce  (£0.65 each)  1      £0.65
cucumber (£0.80 each)  2      £1.60
                 total        £4.60
                              £5.00
                 change       £0.40

        THANK YOU        (7)
```

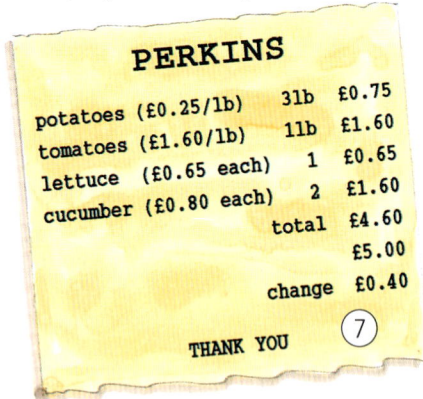

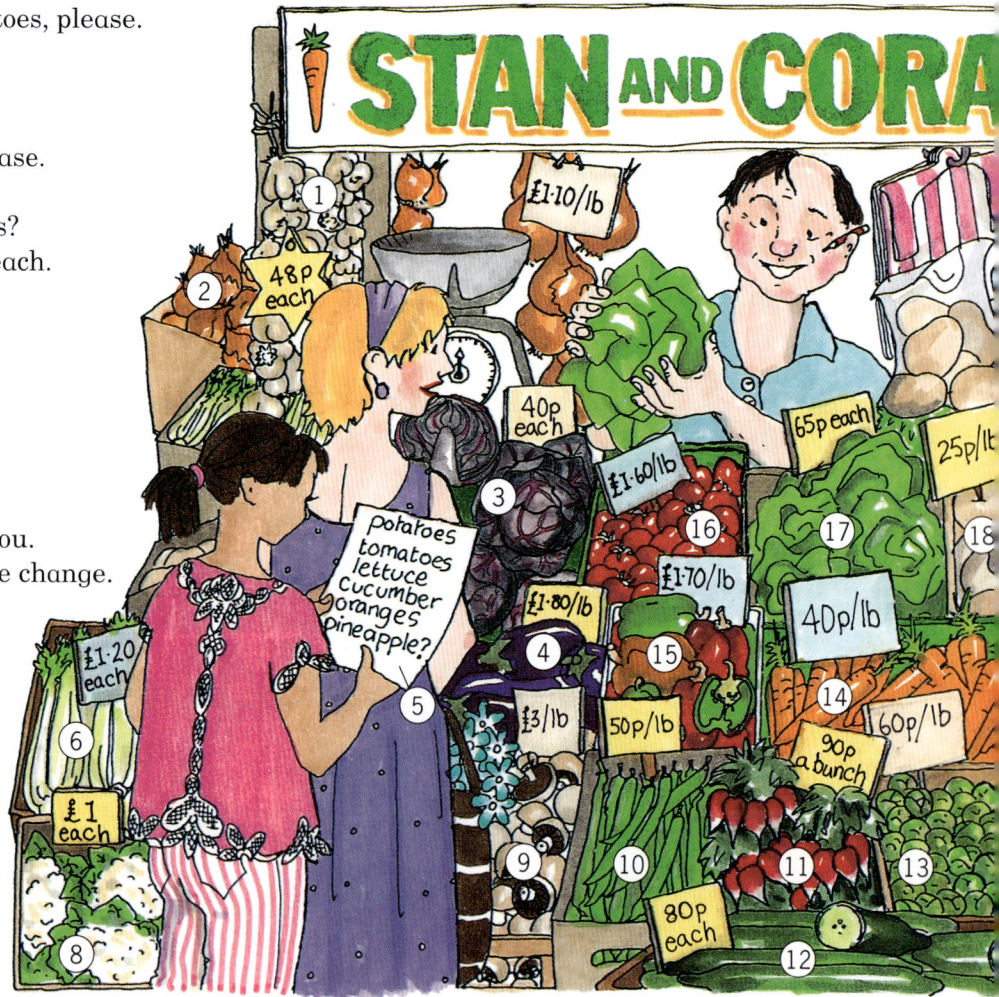

1 garlic	4 aubergine	7 receipt	10 runner bean	13 Brussels sprout	16 tomato
2 onion	5 shopping list	8 cauliflower	11 radish	14 carrot	17 lettuce
3 cabbage	6 celery	9 mushroom	12 cucumber	15 pepper	18 potato

five pounds   five pounds a pound

ten pounds   1 pound = 0.454 kilogram

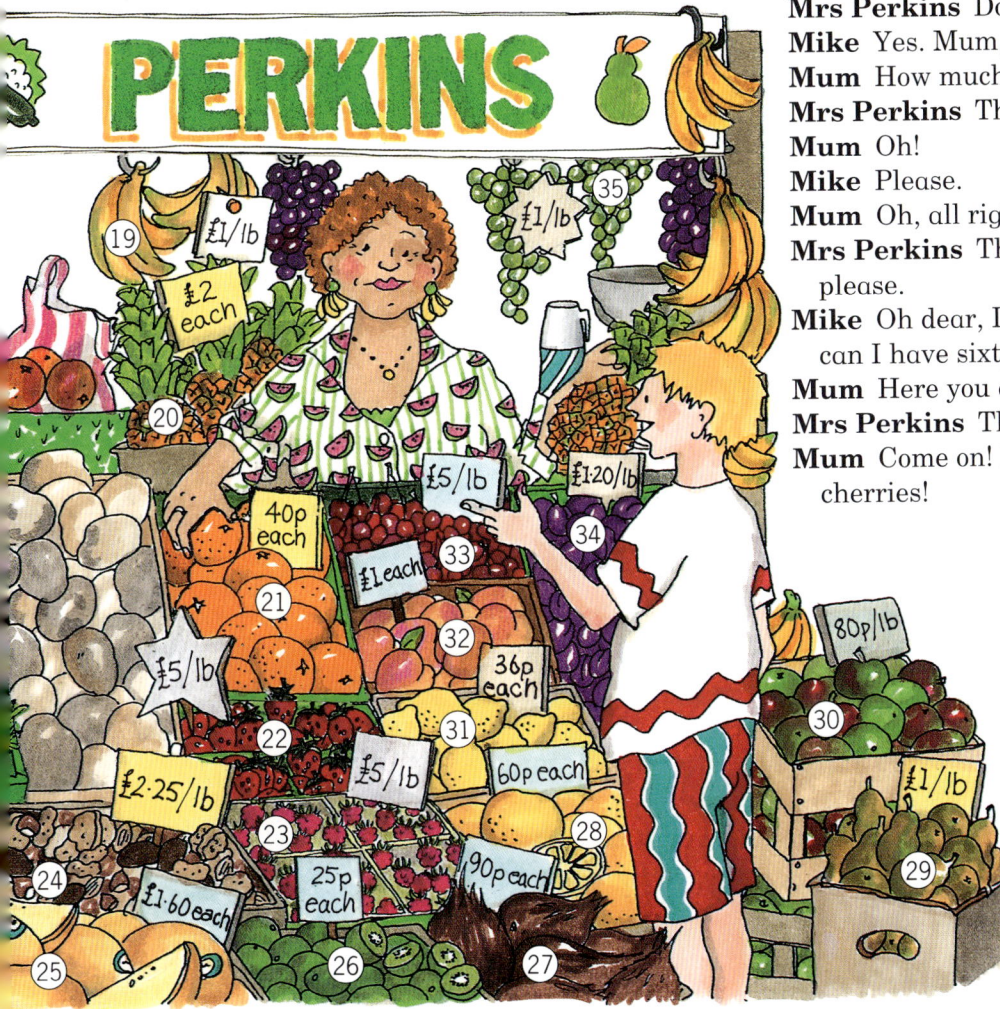

PERKINS

£1/lb

£1/lb

£2 each

40p each

£1 each

£5/lb

£1·20/lb

£5/lb

36p each

£2·25/lb

£5/lb

60p each

25p each

90p each

£1·60 each

80p/lb

£1/lb

£5/lb

Mrs Perkins Hello, Mike.

Mike Hello, Mrs Perkins. Have you got any pineapples today?

Mrs Perkins Yes. Here you are!

Mike Thank you. And four oranges, please.

Mrs Perkins Anything else?

Mike No, thank you. Oh, look at those cherries!

Mrs Perkins Do you like cherries?

Mike Yes. Mum, can we have some cherries?

Mum How much are they?

Mrs Perkins They're five pounds a pound.

Mum Oh!

Mike Please.

Mum Oh, all right. One pound of cherries.

Mrs Perkins That's eight pounds sixty pence, please.

Mike Oh dear, I've only got eight pounds. Mum, can I have sixty pence?

Mum Here you are!

Mrs Perkins Thank you. Goodbye.

Mum Come on! Let's go home and have some cherries!

PERKINS

pineapple(£2.00 each)	1	£2.00
oranges (£0.40 each)	4	£1.60
cherries (£5.00/lb)	1lb	£5.00
	total	£8.60
		£8.60
	change	£0.00

THANK YOU

19 banana	22 strawberry	25 melon	28 grapefruit	31 lemon	34 plum
20 pineapple	23 raspberry	26 kiwi fruit	29 pear	32 peach	35 grape
21 orange	24 nut	27 coconut	30 apple	33 cherry	

THE HAPPY

Mike and Jill are having lunch with Dad, Ben, Tom, and Becky. Everyone is hungry.

Dad I'll have steak, chips, and peas, pancakes, and a cup of coffee. What about you, Ben?

Ben I don't like meat ... I'll have vegetable curry and rice, then cheese and biscuits.

Dad Do you want a cup of coffee?

Ben No, I'd like a cup of tea with sugar, please.

Mike I'll have a hamburger, beans, and chips.

Dad Would you like anything else?

Mike Yes, a yoghurt and a fruit juice ... apple juice, please.

Becky I'd like a salad with brown bread and margarine, and a glass of milk.

Dad What about some ice cream?

Becky No, thanks. I'll have apple pie.

Jill Oh yes, I like apple pie! Can I have apple pie?

Dad Just apple pie?

Jill No, I'd like fish and chips, too, and some white bread and butter.

Dad OK. What would you like to drink?

Jill I'll have mineral water.

Dad What would you like, Tom?

Tom I don't know.

Ben What about spaghetti? You like spaghetti.

Tom No, I had it yesterday.

Dad Oh dear! Aren't you hungry?

Tom Oh yes, I am hungry but ...

Becky Tom likes very funny food.

Dad You can have anything you like.

Tom Well, I'd really like cereal, tomato soup, toast and honey, and some peanuts!

Dad Good! Now everyone's happy. Let's have lunch!

SNAPPER

1 cereal	17 fruit juice	33 fish
2 boiled egg	18 tea	34 chips
3 bread	19 coffee	35 salad
4 bacon and egg	20 sugar	36 pancakes
5 toast	21 soup	37 apple pie
6 roll	22 vegetable curry	38 cream
7 croissant	23 rice	39 cheese and biscuits
8 bun	24 hamburger	40 yoghurt
9 margarine	25 baked beans	41 ice cream
10 butter	26 spaghetti	42 peanuts
11 jam	27 steak	43 biscuits
12 honey	28 peas	44 chocolate
13 milk	29 roast beef	45 sweets
14 milk shake	30 potatoes	46 crisps
15 mineral water	31 chicken	
16 cola	32 sweetcorn	

sausage

hamburger

barbecue

ketchup

hot dog

pizza

sandwich

orange juice

lemonade

birthday cake

candle

birthday card

stereo

jigsaw puzzle

video game

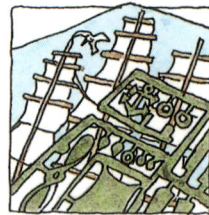
model kit

cassette

It's Mike's birthday. He is ten today and he's having a party in the garden. There are streamers, balloons, and lights in the trees.

There's lots to eat. Dad is cooking sausages and hamburgers on the barbecue. Dad likes lots of ketchup on his hot dogs. Mike's favourite food is pizza. That's on the table with the sandwiches, orange juice, lemonade, and other drinks. Becky is eating crisps. Tom is drinking lemonade and feeding some crisps to Mike's rabbit. Jill is picking up an apple in her mouth from a bowl of water. It's a good game.

Mike has got some birthday cards and lots of presents. He's got a stereo from Mum and Dad, a jigsaw from Jill, a video game, a board game, a model kit, and a kite. Oh no, the kite is in a tree.

Two girls are dancing to Mike's new cassette. Some of the others are playing football. Jill's friends are having a water fight. Here comes Mum with the birthday cake. How many candles? Yes, there are ten. Everybody sings.

'Happy birthday to you.
Happy birthday to you.
Happy birthday, dear Mike.
Happy birthday to you!'

present

kite

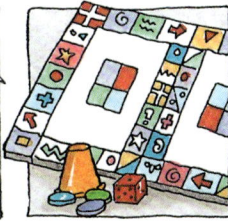
board game

light

balloon

streamer

Mike and Jill do not throw many things away. There isn't much rubbish in their dustbins or in the litter bins at school.

Jill is collecting glass to be recycled. She's taking the lids off the jars and the caps off the bottles. Clear glass goes in the white bin, green goes in the green bin, and brown goes in the brown bin.

Mike and William are collecting cans. Mike is holding a big magnet. There is a recycling bin for tin and another bin for aluminium. Silver paper is made of tin or aluminium too.

Emma is putting things in the plastic recycling bin. She's saving some of the pots and tubs. She washes them and uses them again for plants.

Old envelopes, paper, and newspapers are recycled. John is not putting the magazines in the bin. He is collecting them for his dentist.

Mike's teacher is putting toys and clothes into cardboard boxes. She gives them to the hospital. She uses very old clothes as rags for painting.

A little girl is giving Jill an old bottle.
Jill No, you can take this bottle back to the shop. They wash it and use it again. That's the best kind of recycling.

throw away

recycle

rubbish

dustbin

litter bin

recycling bin

plastic

pot

tub

paper

envelope

newspaper

magazine

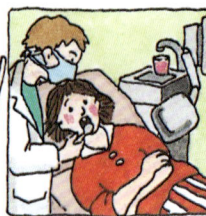

dentist

hospital

can

magnet

silver paper

lid

cap

glass

clothes

cardboard box

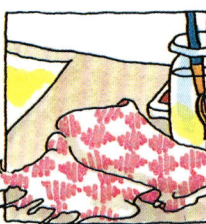

rag

jar

bottle

shop

Mike's class is learning about machines. For homework Mike is asking two families about the machines they have in their homes.

First he asks Mum's friends, Sue and Tony. Then he asks his aunt and uncle, Helen and Tim.

Family 1	Sue and Tony
1 washing machine	1
2 lawnmower	0
3 computer	0
4 sewing machine	0
5 personal stereo	0
6 telephone	3
7 radio	1
8 camcorder	1
9 camera	1
10 cassette recorder	1
11 CD player	2
12 video recorder	1
13 television	2
14 vacuum cleaner	1
15 dishwasher	0

16 aerial

17 CD/compact disc

18 wire

19 plug

20 video

21 microphone

22 light bulb

23 switch

24 battery

25 cassette

26 headphones

27 floppy disk

28 keyboard

29 disk drive

30 screen

31 printer

Family 1: Sue and Tony

Sue and Tony have got three telephones and two televisions. They've got a camcorder and a video recorder. They've got two CD players, one in their house and one in their car. They've got one camera, one cassette recorder, and one radio. They haven't got a sewing machine, a personal stereo or a computer. They've got a vacuum cleaner and a washing machine but they haven't got a dishwasher. They haven't got a garden and they haven't got a lawnmower.

Family 2: Helen and Tim

Tim and Helen have got one telephone and one television. They haven't got a CD player but they've got two radios, a cassette recorder, and a personal stereo. There are three cameras in the house. Helen and Tim have got one and their children have got two. They've got a computer and a sewing machine. They haven't got a camcorder or a video recorder. They've got a lawnmower, two vacuum cleaners, and a washing machine but they haven't got a dishwasher.

It's Saturday afternoon. Jill, Mike, and Mum are looking at the entertainments guide in the newspaper.

Jill There's a film at the cinema called 'Vampires Return'. Can we see that?

Mum No, it's a horror film.

Mike What about 'Gun City'? It's a western.

Jill No, I don't like films about cowboys.

Mum There's 'Cartoon Time'. That looks good.

Mike That's Saturday morning only.

Jill Oh, yes. Well, there's a play at the Swan Theatre called 'Murder!'.

Mum Or there's a musical called 'Happy Days'.

Mike What about a concert? There's the Middleton Orchestra - that's classical music. Or there's Johnny and the Astronauts.

Jill They're a good band. That's Johnny in the picture. He plays electric guitar.

cinema

vampire

cowboy

gun

theatre

actor

orchestra

band

electric guitar

SATURDAY ENTERTAINMENTS GUIDE

■ **CINEMA** ■

123 CINEMA TELEPHONE 0860 124963

Vampires Return
FRIDAY, SATURDAY 14.10 17.40 20.15

GUN CITY
STARTS TODAY
SATURDAY, SUNDAY 13.20 15.00 18.30

Cartoon Time
SATURDAY MORNING 11.00

■ **THEATRE** ■

SWAN THEATRE
MURDER!
SATURDAY 14.00 20.00

QUEEN'S THEATRE
HAPPY DAYS
'The audience loved it' DAILY NEWS
LAST NIGHT SATURDAY 19.30

■ **CONCERTS** ■

THE MIDDLETON ORCHESTRA plays music by **BEETHOVEN**
SUMMERTOWN TOWN HALL
SATURDAY 19.00

NEW STREET ROOMS
Johnny and the Astronauts
TONIGHT AT 20.00

1 horror film   3 cartoon   5 musical

2 western   4 play   6 classical concert

SATURDAY ENTERTAINMENTS GUIDE

■ CIRCUS ■

SUMMERTOWN PARK
SATURDAY 14.00 18.00

This circus uses no animals, only people.

COME TO THE CIRCUS!

■ WHAT'S ON TELEVISION? ■
Today's best programmes guide

BBC 1 18.30
Families First ★★
A great new game show for all the family.

THE BROWNS 5
THE SMITHS 10
THE SMITHS   THE BROWNS
(8)

(9)

CHANNEL 4 20.00
Wildlife Special ★★★
A special programme about the wonderful animals and birds of Australia.

BBC 1 19.15
What's so funny? ★
The comedy show that's full of laughs.

(10)
TV3

BBC 2 21.15
Detective X ★★★
In this week's exciting story Detective X goes to New York.

(11)

■ CROSSWORD ■

CLUES ACROSS →
1 Woof!
3 Not 'he'.
6 What time?
7 It's a food.
8 It's a colour.
9 You wear this round your neck.
11 Not 'yes'.
12 Not 'down'.
13 The last part (of a film for example).
14 It's a toy.

CLUES DOWN ↓
1 It can fly.
2 Don't throw it away. Save it to be _____.
3 You can put things on it.
4 Not 'she'.
5 You can put a letter in it.
8 Free time between lessons or work.
10 I can't _____ without my glasses.
11 A fruit with a hard shell.

1	2		3	4	5
		6			
7					
		8			
9					
10				11	
				12	
13		14			

Jill Oh, look! There's a circus. Look at the clown!

Mum We're going to the circus on Wednesday.

Mike What's on television?

Jill There's a new game show called 'Families First'. It's great!

Mum Oh no, I hate game shows!

Mike There's a wildlife programme about Australia. I'd like to see that.

Jill And there's a good comedy show.

Mum There's a detective story after the news.

Mike OK, let's watch television. Jill can watch the game show and the comedy, I'll watch 'Wildlife Special', and we'll all watch 'Detective X'.

Dad Can I have the newspaper now? I want to do the crossword.

Mum Yes, I'm going to read my book.

Jill What's it called?

Mum It's called 'The Game Show Murders'!

circus   acrobat   clown

juggler   audience   detective

news   crossword   book

7 rock concert   9 wildlife programme   10 comedy show

8 game show   11 detective story

I like playing chess. I go to a chess club on Tuesdays and sometimes I play chess with Jill.

I like sewing and knitting too. I'm making a dress for Jill and a sweater for Mike.

I like painting and I like listening to music. I often listen to classical music when I'm sewing or painting.

I love gardening and I'm very pleased with my roses this year.

I like acting. I go to drama club on Fridays and I act in lots of plays. I like singing and dancing too. Our last play was a musical. It was fun!

I like fishing in the river on Sunday mornings and I like rowing too.

I like hiking. I put on my hiking boots and my rucksack and sing as I walk along.

playing chess

needle

cotton

sewing

acting

river

fishing rod

fishing

listening to music

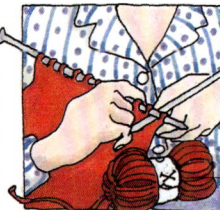

knitting needle

wool

knitting

singing

rowing boat

oar

rowing

painting

gardening

rose

dancing

rucksack

hiking boot

hiking

I like reading. I read about two books a week. I like playing the guitar. I play every day and I have a lesson on Mondays.

I like skateboarding with my friends in the park and I like collecting stamps. I've got about two hundred stamps in my album. Sometimes I like playing cards with Dad and Jill.

Last summer I went on a sailing holiday. It was great! I really like sailing.

I like making models. I'm making a model airport out of old cardboard boxes! I like drawing too. This is a picture of Muddy.

I like playing on the computer and writing letters to my friends. I've got one friend in London, one friend in Spain, and one friend in Australia.

I like skating in the park and, now I've got a new bike, I like cycling too.

reading

skateboarding

knee-pad

skateboard

making models

model plane

drawing

playing the guitar

collecting stamps

album

stamp

picture

playing on the computer

writing letters

playing cards

sailing

roller skates

roller skating

cycling

helmet

bicycle/bike

Jill and Mike are at the sports centre. They are looking at people doing different sports.

Jill and Mike play football, cricket, netball, rounders, volleyball, tennis, and hockey at school. Mike is in the school football team. They do athletics and gymnastics at school too. Jill likes gymnastics. They go swimming every week and Mike is good at diving. Jill can swim but she can't dive.

Mike goes to a judo club after school and Jill sometimes plays table tennis at their cousins' house.

Their cousin, Becky, goes riding. She loves horses. Their cousin, Ben, does karate. He plays rugby too. Some of Jill and Mike's friends go skiing.

Mum plays badminton and Dad sometimes plays squash. Dad likes watching basketball on television. Sometimes all the family go to watch motor racing. It's very noisy.

Jill and Mike watch boxing and wrestling on television. Sometimes they watch baseball too.

Jill's teacher, Mr Benn, goes hang-gliding at weekends. Mike's teacher goes canoeing.

What a lot of different sports! Jill and Mike would like to try them all.

rounders   hockey   netball

basketball

volleyball

cricket

athletics

tennis

squash

badminton

swimming

diving

rugby

motor racing

skiing

riding

hang-gliding

canoeing

baseball

football team

football

1 base

2 hockey stick

3 net

4 racket

5 tennis court

6 shuttlecock

7 swimming pool

8 racing car

9 ski

10 horse

11 hang-glider

12 canoe

13 paddle

14 bat

15 goal

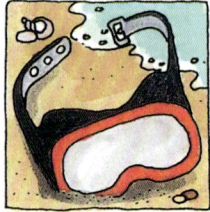
goggles

sunglasses

flipper

snorkel

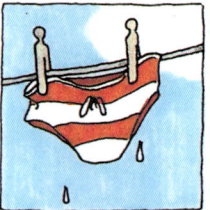
swimming trunks

swimsuit

sunbather

beach umbrella

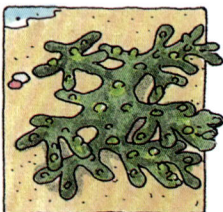
seaweed

shell

sand

sandcastle

bucket

spade

windsurfer

seagull

cliff

Jill, Mike, and their cousins are at the seaside. Everybody is on the beach or in the sea.

Mike is sitting on a rock looking through his binoculars. He can see a ship, a lighthouse, and some seagulls. There's a boat and a water-skier. It's Auntie Sarah! She's very good. Uncle Paul is windsurfing with Ben. They aren't very good. Jill and Mum are swimming. Muddy wants to swim too but he doesn't like the waves.

Tom is making a big sandcastle for baby Lucy. Lucy is playing with a bucket and spade. She loves the sand. Tom is putting shells and seaweed on the sandcastle. It looks good.

Auntie Helen is sunbathing. She's wearing a blue swimsuit and sunglasses. Uncle Tim is sitting under a beach umbrella. He doesn't like the sun.

Becky is running and shouting. 'There's something in the cave', she shouts. 'It's something scary!'

Everybody looks at the cave at the bottom of the cliff. Someone is coming out. He's wearing swimming trunks, flippers, a snorkel, and goggles. It's Dad! He's going snorkelling.

cave

beach

sea

binoculars

lighthouse

ship

boat

water-skier

wave

rock

41   the travel game

Mike and Jill are going to France. They are playing 'The Travel Game'. Mike takes a card and Jill takes a card. Mike's card says 'coach'. He looks for a coach. Jill's card says 'bicycle'.

'There's a bicycle', says Jill. Jill scores five points and takes another card. Jill's next card says 'lorry'. They stop at a filling station to get some petrol.

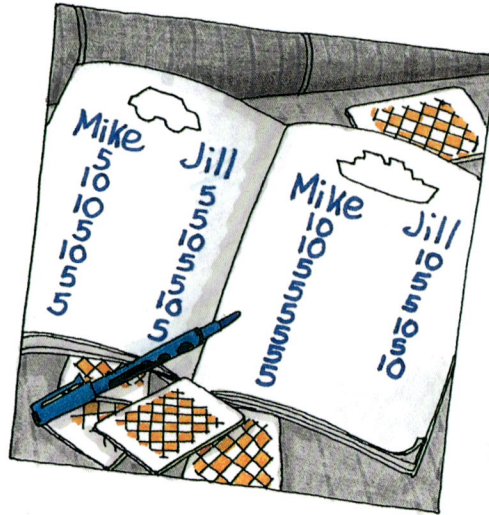

They see a van, a motorbike, and lots of cars - but no coaches and no lorries. The first player to score fifty points wins the game. Can you see who wins?

They play on the ferry. Jill looks for a hydrofoil and Mike looks for a hovercraft. Then Jill looks for a yacht and Mike looks for a liner.

Can you see who wins on the ferry?

1 filling station	4 engine	7 tyre	10 headlight	13 chain	16 saddle
2 petrol pump	5 boot	8 windscreen	11 number plate	14 pedal	17 handlebar
3 bonnet	6 wheel	9 steering wheel	12 spokes	15 pump	

the travel game 5 points	the travel game 5 points	the travel game 10 points	the travel game 10 points	the travel game 10 points
oil tanker	container ship	liner	hovercraft	lifeboat

the travel game 5 points	the travel game 5 points	the travel game 5 points	the travel game 10 points	the travel game 10 points
yacht	motor boat	fishing boat	hydrofoil	ferry

the travel game 5 points	the travel game 5 points	the travel game 5 points	the travel game 10 points	the travel game 10 points
bicycle	motorbike	van	pick-up truck	jeep

the travel game 5 points	the travel game 5 points	the travel game 10 points	the travel game 10 points	the travel game 10 points
lorry	coach	caravan	ambulance	fire engine

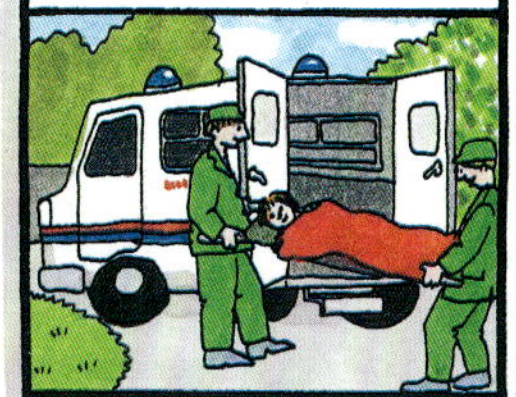

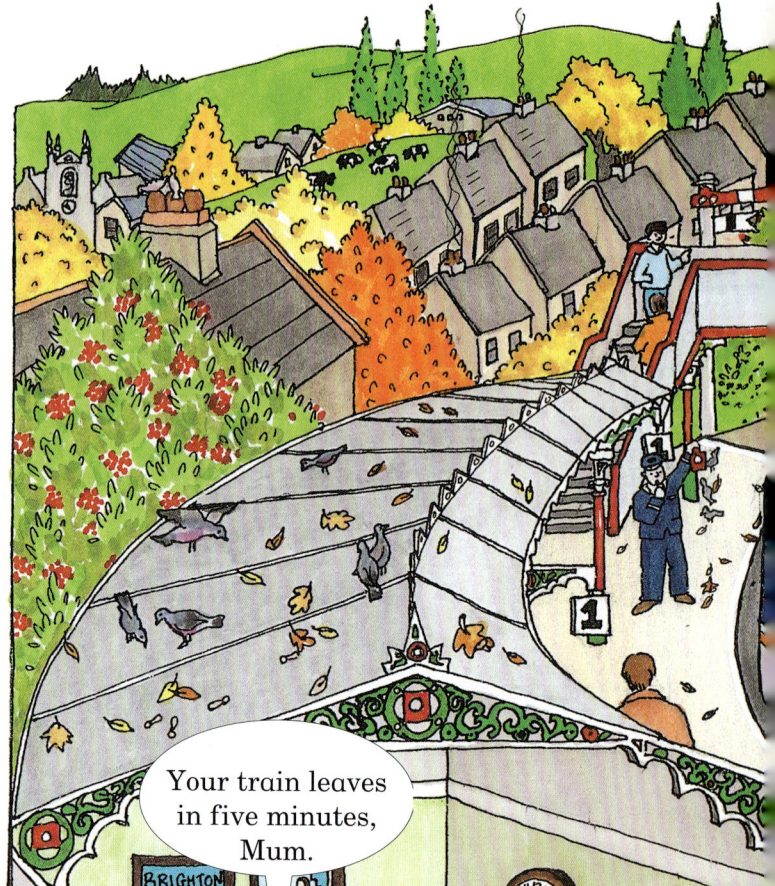

Mike, Jill, Mum, and Granny are at the station. Granny is going to London to see her sister.

Mum is standing in a queue at the ticket office. She's waiting to buy Granny's ticket. Mike is carrying Granny's suitcase and Jill is carrying her bag.

There's a train in the station now. There are lots of passengers on the train. All the coaches are full. A ticket collector is taking tickets. Here comes Mike's friend, William, with his rucksack.

Granny is looking at the timetable. 'I think my train leaves at ten o'clock', she says.

The guard blows his whistle and the engine starts.

train   coach   engine   ticket   ticket office   queue

tunnel

bridge

driver

track

platform

seat

guard

whistle

timetable

suitcase

bag

rucksack

ticket collector

passenger

kiss

wave

car park

luggage

check-in

passport control

security

duty-free shop

departure lounge

ticket

boarding card

passport

security officer

X-ray machine

perfume

Auntie Sarah, Uncle Paul, and baby Lucy are going to Jamaica to see Sarah's grandmother.

Mum, Mike, and Jill take them to the airport. Mum parks the car in the car park and eveybody goes to the check-in. The man at the check-in looks at Sarah's, Paul's, and Lucy's tickets, takes their luggage, and gives them their boarding cards. Sarah and Paul look at their boarding cards to see their seat numbers on the plane.

Mum, Mike, and Jill say 'Goodbye!' to Sarah, Paul, and Lucy at passport control. Jill kisses Lucy and waves to her. They show their passports and then go through security. A security officer checks their bags with an X-ray machine. They go into the departure lounge to wait for their flight. Sarah buys some perfume for her grandmother at the duty-free shop.

Mike and Jill are watching the planes. They can see the runway and the control tower. A helicopter is landing and a plane is taking off. It's Uncle Paul and Auntie Sarah's plane.

1 cockpit

2 pilot

3 cabin

4 steward

5 helicopter

6 plane

7 tail

8 wing

9 jet engine

10 nose

11 runway

control tower

take-off

landing

customs

In ten hours the pilot lands the plane in Jamaica. They go through passport control, collect their luggage, then go through customs. Sarah's grandmother is waiting for them.

Jill, Mike, and Mum are going to a magic castle.

They sit in a little car. The car goes into the castle. There's a king and a queen, and two knights. The king and the queen are wearing crowns. The knights are wearing armour. One knight has a sword and a shield. The other knight has a big axe. He looks frightening.

Now there's a wizard and a witch. The witch has a black cat, a broomstick, and a cauldron. The wizard has a silver cloak and a magic wand.

The car goes into a giant's room. Everything is big here. There's a big table, a big chair, and a big foot. It's the giant's foot.

The car goes through a door. Now they're in fairyland. There's nothing frightening here. There are flowers and fairies everywhere.

The car goes into a cave. There's a dinosaur, a dragon, and lots of different monsters.

The car goes onto a pirate ship. The pirates have got a treasure chest. A door opens and the car goes into the moat. Splash! There's water everywhere.

castle

moat

king

queen

crown

sword

shield

knight

armour

axe

witch

broomstick

cauldron

wizard

magic wand

cloak

giant

fairy

dinosaur

dragon

monster

pirate

treasure chest

card

heart

violet

rose

Saint Valentine's Day: 14 February

On Saint Valentine's Day we send a card to the person we love. We don't write our name in the card. Sometimes the cards have hearts on them. People give presents too. Dad gave Mum a red rose. It means 'I love you'.

Easter egg

hot cross bun

Easter Day: a Sunday in March or April

We call the Friday before Easter 'Good Friday'. On Good Friday we eat hot cross buns. Sometimes they are cold but we still call them 'hot cross buns'! On Easter Day we all have chocolate Easter eggs. They're lovely!

mask

pumpkin

ghost

skeleton

Hallowe'en: 31 October

Some people think that ghosts come out at night on Hallowe'en. At Hallowe'en parties people wear frightening clothes and masks. In this picture I'm a ghost and Mike is a skeleton. We make a face from a pumpkin and put a candle in it. Then we put it in the window to frighten people.

guy

bonfire

firework

Guy Fawkes

blow up

Houses of Parliament

Bonfire Night: 5 November

On 5 November 1605 a man called Guy Fawkes tried to blow up the Houses of Parliament in London. Now on 'Bonfire Night' we have bonfires and lots of fireworks. We make a 'guy' from old clothes and put it on the bonfire.

Father Christmas

Christmas tree

Christmas Day: 25 December

At Christmas we send Christmas cards to everyone we know. We put decorations everywhere and we have a Christmas tree with an angel on the top. We call 24 December 'Christmas Eve'. On Christmas Eve Father Christmas puts presents in our Christmas stockings. On Christmas Day there are presents for everyone. We eat turkey, Christmas pudding, and Christmas cake. Muddy loves Christmas!

Christmas card

decorations

angel

turkey

Christmas pudding

Christmas cake

a Christmas carol

We wish you a merry Christmas, we wish you a merry Christmas, we wish you a merry Christmas, and a happy new year!

51 Muddy's year

Muddy the dog goes for a walk every day of the year, in spring, in summer, in autumn, and in winter. He likes some months better than others.

in spring, in summer,

January

snowball
snowman
snow

It's winter and it's snowing. I like snow but I don't like snowballs!

February

umbrella
rain

It's raining. Mike's got an umbrella but I haven't! I don't like the rain. Let's go home!

March

wind
grass
daffodil

It's spring. There are daffodils in the grass. It's very windy.

April

sun
rainbow

It's raining and the sun is shining. There's a rainbow!

May

tree
blossom

It's warm today and there's blossom on the trees. Oh look, there's my friend, Sam!

June

sky
strawberry

It's summer. The sky is blue. It's a sunny day. Jill and Mike are picking strawberries. I don't like strawberries. I like ice cream.

in autumn, and in winter

July

leaf

leaves

It's hot today. I don't want to run. I like sitting under this tree and eating ice cream.

August

BANG

thunder

lightning

There are black clouds in the sky. Oh no, there's some thunder and lightning. I hate thunderstorms.

September

bushes

bush

berries

berry

The leaves are red, yellow, and brown and there are berries in the bushes. It's autumn.

October

cloud

toadstool

It's cloudy today. What's this? It's a toadstool.

November

fog

It's foggy. Can you see me in this fog? I can't see anything.

December

puddle

ice

It's winter now. There's ice on the puddles. My feet are cold. What's your favourite season? I like summer best.

open/closed

heavy/light

dry/wet

cold/hot

fat/thin

tall/short

strong/weak

beautiful/ugly

long/short

curly/straight

young/old

tidy/untidy

high/low

quiet/noisy

narrow/wide

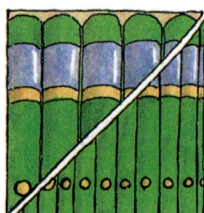
thick/thin

big/small

empty/full

alive/dead

fast/slow

hard/soft

rough/smooth

bitter/sweet

light/dark

old/new

blunt/sharp

clean/dirty

cheap/expensive

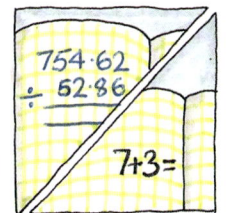
difficult/easy

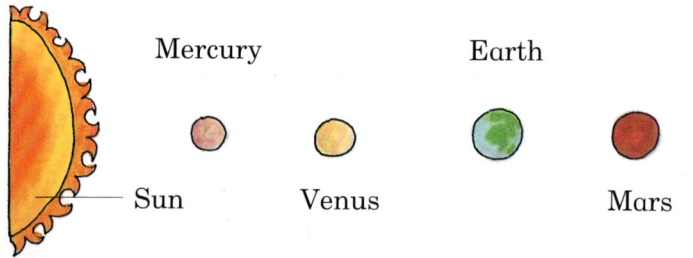

Mercury   Earth

Sun   Venus   Mars

Jill is playing on her computer. The game is called 'Space Adventure'. She's very good at it!

astronaut

spacesuit

blast off

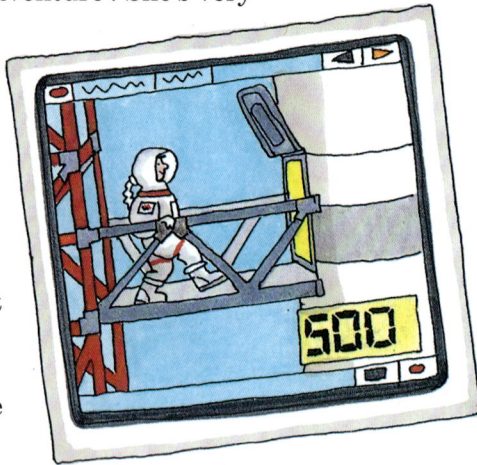

The little astronaut puts on his spacesuit and runs to the launch pad. There is a space shuttle. Jill's astronaut gets into the space shuttle. Jill gets 500 points.

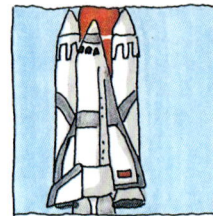

rocket

space shuttle

launch pad

satellite

earth

orbit

ZOOM! The space shuttle blasts off into space. Both rockets are working. Jill gets 500 more points.

There are lots of satellites orbiting the earth. CRASH! Oh, no! The space shuttle hits one of the satellites. Jill loses 100 points.

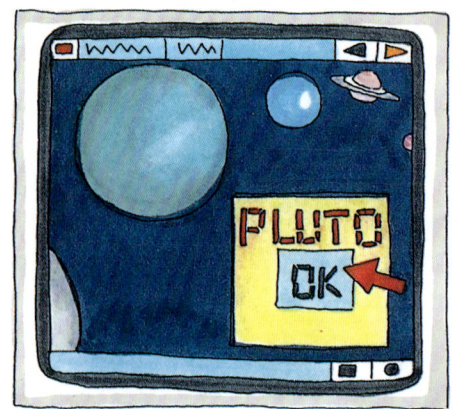

Now the astronaut can visit one of the nine planets. Which one? Jill chooses Pluto. Jill's astronaut goes to Pluto and Jill gets 1000 more points.

Jupiter   Uranus   Pluto

Saturn   Neptune

sun

moon

planet

It's time for Jill to go to bed. She looks out of the window. The moon is shining and there are lots of stars in the sky. Everything is quiet. It is very different from Jill's computer game.

spaceship

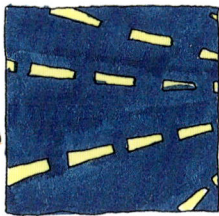
shine

star

alien

shoot

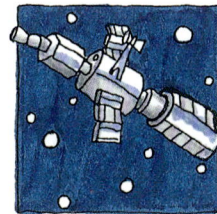
space station

Oh, no! There are space aliens on the planet. They don't look friendly. Jill's astronaut runs to the space shuttle and blasts off. ZOOM! Jill gets 500 points.

The aliens are in spaceships now. They're shooting at Jill's astronaut. POW! POW! POW! He goes to a friendly space station. He's safe! Jill gets 1000 points.

ZOOM! The astronaut is going back to earth. He doesn't land on the houses. He doesn't land on the trees. SPLASH! He lands in the sea. The game finishes and the music plays.

Becky is having a party. Everyone is from another country. Becky is giving everyone a flag with the name of their country on it.

Becky Which country do you come from, Mike?

Mike I come from Egypt. Where do you come from?

Becky Guess!

Mike I don't know. Which continent is it in?

Becky It's in Europe.

Mike Is it Sweden?

Becky No.

Mike Is it Poland?

Becky No. Look at my feet!

Mike Oh, you're from the Netherlands.

Becky That's right! I'm from the Netherlands. Ben's from Mexico. Look at his hat! Tom's from India. Where do you come from, Jill?

Jill I'm from Greenland.

Becky I haven't got a flag for Greenland.

Jill Greenland is part of Denmark. Have you got a flag for Denmark?

Becky Yes, here it is. Oh, hello, Muddy, what are you doing here?

Jill He's come to the party. Look at his collar. He's from America!

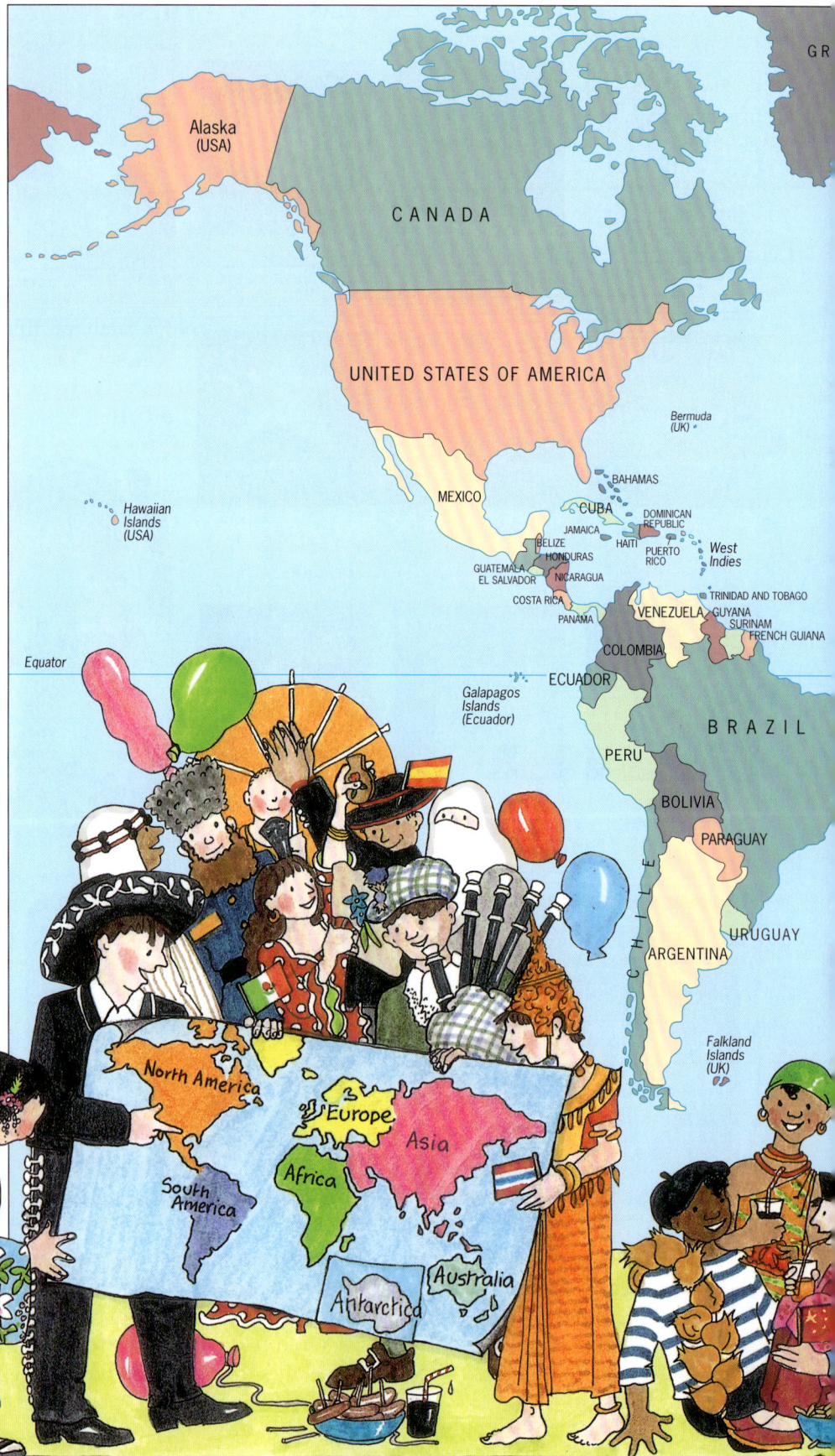

Alaska (USA) — CANADA — UNITED STATES OF AMERICA — Bermuda (UK) — Hawaiian Islands (USA) — MEXICO — BAHAMAS — CUBA — DOMINICAN REPUBLIC — JAMAICA — HAITI — PUERTO RICO — West Indies — BELIZE — HONDURAS — GUATEMALA — EL SALVADOR — NICARAGUA — COSTA RICA — PANAMA — TRINIDAD AND TOBAGO — VENEZUELA — GUYANA — SURINAM — FRENCH GUIANA — COLOMBIA — ECUADOR — Galapagos Islands (Ecuador) — Equator — BRAZIL — PERU — BOLIVIA — PARAGUAY — CHILE — URUGUAY — ARGENTINA — Falkland Islands (UK) — GR

North America — Europe — Asia — Africa — South America — Australia — Antarctica

ICELAND

Faeroe Islands (Denmark)

RUSSIAN FEDERATION (RUSSIA)

NORWAY SWEDEN FINLAND

ESTONIA
LATVIA

UNITED KINGDOM
DENMARK
IRISH REPUBLIC
LI
BELARUS
GERMANY POLAND
N
B
CZ
UKRAINE
LU
AU H R MOLDAVIA
FRANCE
S SLA
ITALY BH Y
BULGARIA
GEORGIA
PORTUGAL SPAIN
E
GREECE
TURKEY
AR AZ
KAZAKHSTAN
UZBEKISTAN
TU
MONGOLIA
NORTH KOREA
JAPAN
K
T
CHINA
SOUTH KOREA

PORTUGAL SPAIN
Azores (Portugal)
Canary Islands (Spain)
TUNISIA
CYPRUS LEBANON ISRAEL
SYRIA
IRAN
AFGHANISTAN
disputed area
MOROCCO
IRAQ
KUWAIT
BAHRAIN
PAKISTAN
NEPAL BHUTAN
MYANMAR (BURMA)
Taiwan
WESTERN SAHARA
ALGERIA LIBYA EGYPT
JORDAN
Q
SAUDI ARABIA
INDIA
Hong Kong (UK)
MAURITANIA
UAE
OMAN
MALI NIGER CHAD
ERITREA
BANGLADESH
LAOS
SENEGAL
G
SUDAN
YEMEN REPUBLIC
DJIBOUTI
Socotra (Yemen Republic)
THAILAND
VIETNAM
PHILIPPINES
G-B GUINEA
BU
BE NIGERIA
SRI LANKA
CAMBODIA BRUNEI DARUSSALAM
SIERRA LEONE
GHANA
CAR
ETHIOPIA
SOMALIA
MALAYSIA
LIBERIA
CÔTE D'IVOIRE (IVORY COAST)
TOGO CAMEROON
EQUATORIAL GUINEA
ZAÏRE
U KENYA
MALDIVES
SINGAPORE
Equator
SAO TOMÉ AND PRINCIPE
GABON
CONGO
RWANDA BURUNDI
TANZANIA
INDONESIA
Ascension Island (UK)
MALAWI
SOLOMON ISLANDS
PAPUA NEW GUINEA
TUVALU
St Helena (UK)
ANGOLA ZAMBIA
COMOROS
VANUATU
FIJI
NAMIBIA ZM MOZAMBIQUE MADAGASCAR
AUSTRALIA
New Caledonia (France)
BOTSWANA
SWAZILAND
SOUTH AFRICA LESOTHO
NEW ZEALAND

small countries on this map

A	ALBANIA
AR	ARMENIA
AU	AUSTRIA
AZ	AZERBAIJAN
B	BELGIUM
BE	BENIN
BH	BOSNIA-HERZEGOVINA
BU	BURKINA
C	CROATIA
CAR	CENTRAL AFRICAN REPUBLIC
CZ	CZECH REPUBLIC
F	FYROM Former Yugoslav Republic of Macedonia
G	GAMBIA
G-B	GUINEA-BISSAU
H	HUNGARY
K	KIRGYZSTAN
LI	LITHUANIA
LU	LUXEMBOURG
N	NETHERLANDS
Q	QATAR
R	ROMANIA
S	SWITZERLAND
SL	SLOVENIA
SLA	SLOVAKIA
T	TAJIKISTAN
TU	TURKMENISTAN
U	UGANDA
UAE	UNITED ARAB EMIRATES
Y	YUGOSLAVIA
ZM	ZIMBABWE

The postman is bringing lots of postcards today.
Can you match the words to the pictures?

Dear Jill and Mike,
We're staying with our uncle and aunt in Northern Ireland. They live in a big house by the sea. Yesterday we went riding on the beach.
Love,
Becky and Tom.

Jill and Mike Robinson
21 Ashgrove Road
Summertown
England

NEWCASTLE 7 PM 15 AUG 1999

Dear Anna and David,
The island is very quiet. There are lots of birds and not many people. We like it very much!
Love to everyone,
granny and grandad

Arran, off the west coast of Scotland

Mr and Mrs D. Robinson and family,
21 Ashgrove Road
Summertown
England

ISLE OF ARRAN 5 PM 16 AUG 1999

Dear Mike,
I'm staying in the capital of Scotland. It's great! We saw this castle yesterday. It's on the top of a hill in the middle of the city. It's very old.
See you soon,
William

Mike Robinson
21 Ashgrove Road
Summertown
England

EDINBURGH 7·45 PM 17 AUG 1999

Dear Jill,
Today we went to Land's End. There are signposts pointing to other countries. We looked west but we couldn't see America!
Love, Emma
xxx

Jill Robinson,
21 Ashgrove Road
Summertown

PENZANCE 7 AM 16 AUG 1999

Dear Jill and Mike,
This is a picture of the mountain I climbed yesterday. Grandma went up on the train but I walked. (I came down on the train!)
Love, Grandpa

Mount Snowdon is the highest mountain in Wales.

Jill and Mike Robinson
21 Ashgrove Road
Summertown
England

LLANBERIS 4·30 PM 17 AUG 1999

Dear Jill and Mike,
This is the town where Shakespeare was born. Yesterday we saw his house, his church, and his school. Then we went on a boat on the river. Lucy liked the river best!
Lots of love,
Paul, Sarah, and Lucy

Jill and Mike Robinson
21 Ashgrove Road
Summertown

STRATFORD-UPON-AVON 11·30 AM 17 AUG 1999

signpost

lake

hill

mountain

island

town

north

north-west   north-east

west   east

south-west   south-east

south

- town
- city
- ■ capital city
- ~ river
- lake
- ▲ top of a hill or mountain
- hill
- mountain

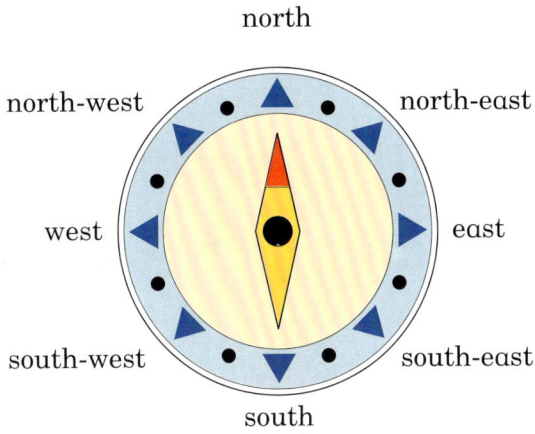

Shetland Islands

Orkney Islands

Outer Hebrides

Skye
Inverness
Spey
Dee
Aberdeen
Ben Nevis 1344 m
Mull
Tay
Dundee
Islay
Glasgow
Clyde
Arran
Edinburgh
Tweed

Belfast
Slieve Donard 852 m
Newcastle
Isle of Man
Douglas
Erne
Tyne
Newcastle
Tees
Scafell Pike 978 m
Middlesbrough
York
Bradford
Leeds
Hull
Shannon
Anglesey
Liverpool
Manchester
Aire
Sheffield
Dublin
Llanberis
Snowdon 1085 m
Stoke-on-Trent
Barrow
Trent
Derby
Nottingham
Norwich
Birmingham
Leicester
Blackwater
Carrauntoohill 1041 m
Coventry
Avon
Great Ouse
Cambridge
Severn
Wye
Stratford-upon-Avon
Ipswich
Cork
coast
Gloucester
Oxford
Swansea
Thames
London
Cardiff
Bristol
Reading
Southampton
Brighton
Dover
Poole
Portsmouth
Isle of Wight
Plymouth
Land's End
Isles of Scilly
Penzance

city

SCOTLAND
NORTHERN IRELAND
IRISH REPUBLIC
WALES
ENGLAND

Our aunt, Jenny, lives in London. One weekend we went to stay with her and she took us sightseeing.

On Saturday we went to Buckingham Palace. We saw the soldiers but we didn't see the Queen. Then we went to Trafalgar Square and fed the pigeons. After lunch we went to the Natural History Museum. We stayed there all afternoon. There were lots of things to see. I liked the dinosaurs best. Then we went back to Jenny's house on the tube.

On Sunday morning we went to see the Houses of Parliament and Big Ben. We heard Big Ben strike eleven. Then we went on a boat on the River Thames. We saw lots of bridges. My favourite was Tower Bridge.

After lunch we went to the Tower of London. The buildings there are very old. The White Tower was built in 1078. We saw the Beefeaters and the Crown Jewels. At the end of the afternoon we were very tired. We went back to Jenny's house in a taxi.

It was a lovely weekend.

Buckingham Palace

soldier

busby

Trafalgar Square

Nelson's Column

statue

Saturday

This is Mike outside Buckingham Palace. It's the Queen's house in London. The soldier is wearing a hat called a 'busby'. It looks very hot.

This is Trafalgar Square. There's a statue of Nelson on 'Nelson's Column', some statues of lions, some fountains, and lots of pigeons!

This is me and a dinosaur at the Natural History Museum.

This is Mike and Jenny on the escalator in the underground station. Londoners call the underground the 'tube'.

Sunday

This is my photo of Big Ben. 'Big Ben' is really the name of the bell inside the clock.

fountain

pigeon

museum

This is Mike and me on the boat by Tower Bridge.

escalator

the tube / the underground

Big Ben

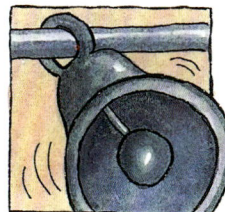

bell

Houses of Parliament

These are the soldiers at the Tower of London. They're called 'Beefeaters'. Mike's in the picture too - he's the one in a T-shirt!

Tower Bridge

River Thames

Beefeater

This is Jenny and a London taxi.

The Tower of London

The Crown Jewels

The White Tower

left

Jill, Mike, and their cousins are on a treasure hunt. Mike's got the first clue. But where is clue number two? And where is the treasure? (The 'treasure' is their picnic lunch!)

clue 3: Go along the footpath to the stream. Look for a bridge.

clue 6: Go along the road to the crossroads. Look for a road sign.

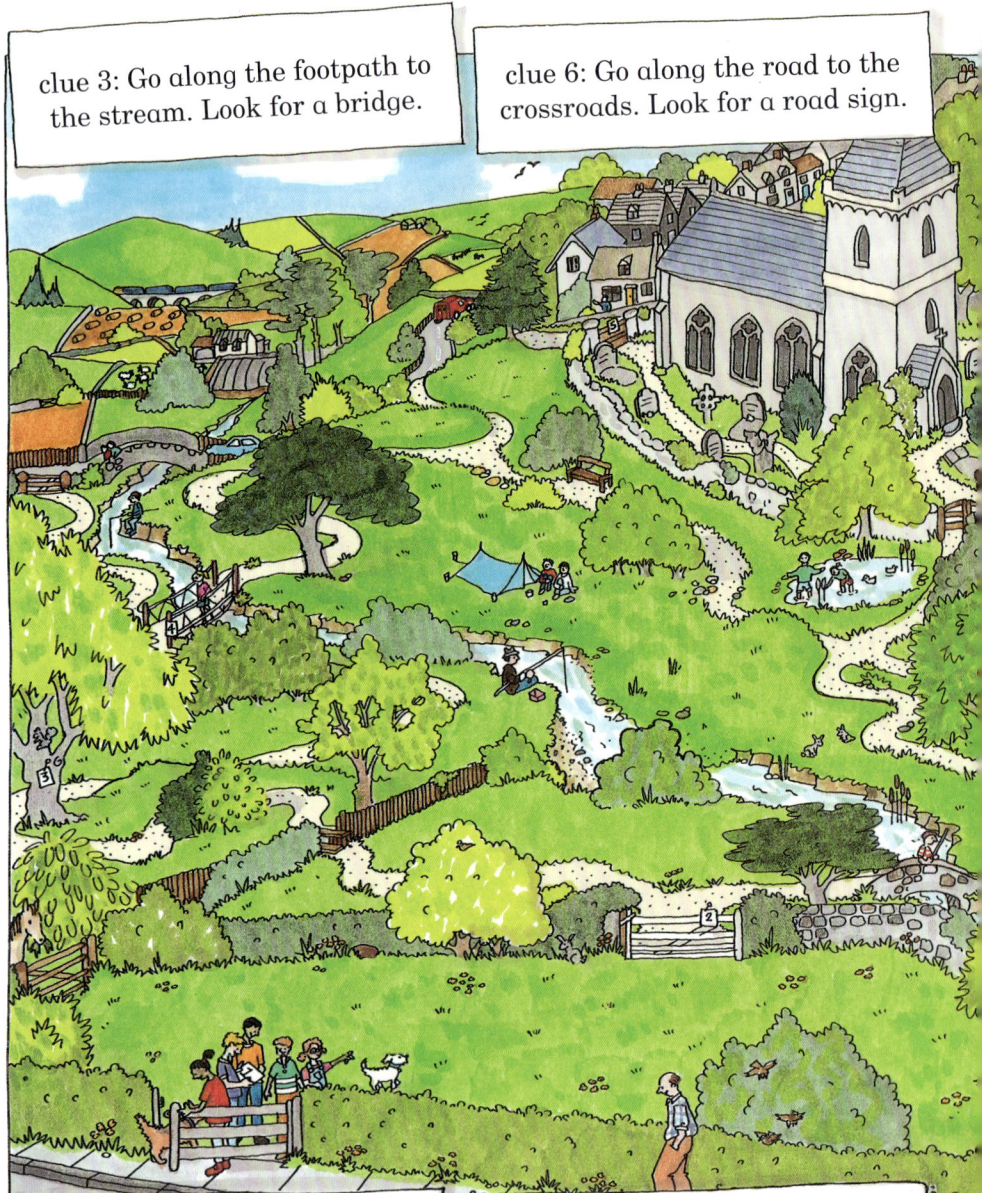

clue 1: Go across the field to the white gate.

clue 4: Go over the bridge and up the hill to the church gate.

clue 9: Turn left and go out of the wood. Look for a ladder.

clue 2: Go through the gate and turn left. Look for a big tree.

clue 8: Go into the wood. Look for a seat.

clue 10: Go up the ladder and look for ... the treasure!

stream

footpath

crossroads

road sign

seat

ladder

field

wood

right

clue 5: Go round the church and turn right onto the road. Look for a postbox.

clue 7: Turn off the road. Go down the hill towards the wood. Look for some flowers.

church

round the church

across the field

over the bridge

up the hill   down the hill

to the gate

through the gate

towards the wood

into the wood

out of the wood

turn onto the road   go along the road   turn off the road

farm

farmer

barn

hay

tractor

donkey

horse   foal

pig   piglet

sheep   lamb

Jill's class and their teacher, Mr Benn, are visiting a farm.

Jill likes the horses best. The brown horse has a foal. It's called 'Moonlight'. Emma is feeding the chickens. The geese and the ducks are hungry too. Max is looking at the cows. There are two calves. They are ten days old. Charles likes the pigs. He thinks they're funny!

The farmer is driving his tractor. He's taking hay to the barn. 'Here are some apples,' he says. 'Give them to the goats and the donkey. But don't give them to the bull. He's not friendly!'

Jill sees the farmer's sheepdog, Bess. 'Where are the sheep?' she asks.

'In the field behind the hedge,' says the farmer. 'The lambs are playing by the bushes.'

'Where's Mr Benn?' says Emma.

'He's by the pond,' says Jill.

Mr Benn is sitting under a tree. It's a hot day. Mr Benn's jacket is on a branch.

'Mr Benn! Mr Benn!' say the children. 'Come and look at the horses, ... the goats, ... the tractor, ... the pigs!' But Mr Benn doesn't answer. He's asleep.

goat

sheepdog

pond

branch

goose

duck

chicken

cow

calf

bull

This is 'The Land of Animals Safari Park'. It's in England but the animals come from other countries.

Jill and Mike and their parents are driving through it.

In 'Lion Land' a lion with a big mane is sleeping. Other lions are licking their paws.

lion

mane

The wolves in 'Wolf Wood' look like dogs with grey fur. One wolf is digging. 'Muddy likes digging too,' says Jill.

paw

claw

wolf

fur

In 'Elephant Land' an elephant is using his trunk to have a shower! There's a rhinoceros by the water too.

'Where are the tigers?' says Jill. 'Oh, there's one in the tree!'

elephant

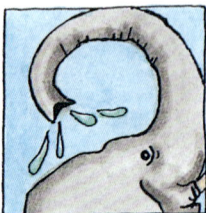
trunk

tusk

rhinoceros

horn

tiger

'We can't leave the Safari Park!'

'We've got two monkeys in the back of the car!'

'Why not?'

Four long legs walk past the window. It's a giraffe! There are deer, antelopes, zebras, camels and ostriches here too.

In 'Monkey Land' a monkey sits on the car. There's a buffalo there too. 'Look at those big horns!' says Mum.

'What are those birds with pink feathers?' asks Jill. They're flamingos,' says Mike. 'But I can't see a hippo, can you?'

monkey

buffalo

flamingo

feather

camel

gorilla

ostrich

leopard

hippopotamus

cheetah

giraffe

antelope

deer

zebra

69 animals

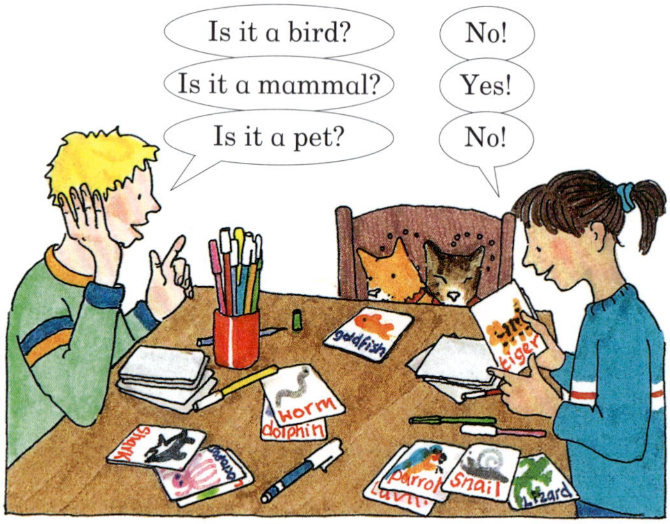

Is it a bird?
No!
Is it a mammal?
Yes!
Is it a pet?
No!
goldfish
tiger
worm
dolphin
parrot
snail
lizard

Jill and Mike are playing 'The Animal Game'. Jill draws a picture of an animal. Mike can't see it. Mike tries to guess the animal. He asks Jill ten questions. Jill answers 'yes' or 'no'. Then Mike draws an animal and Jill asks the questions.

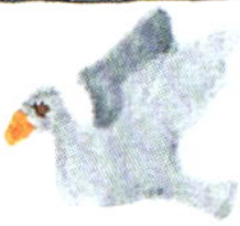
bird

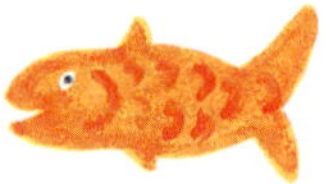
fish

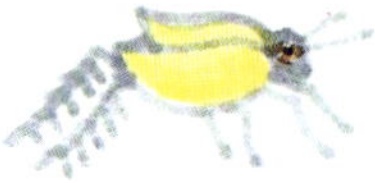
insect

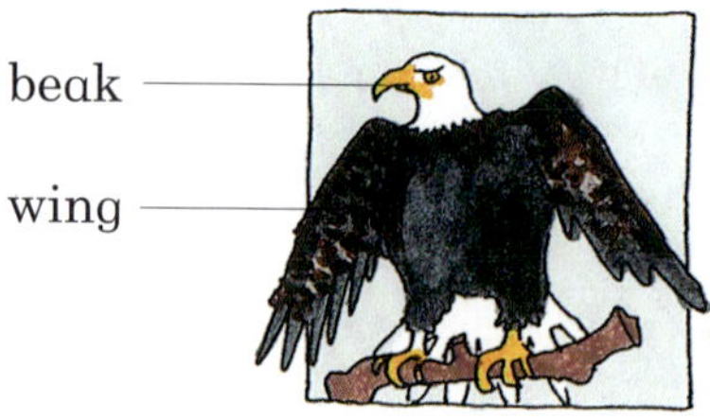

beak
wing

eagle

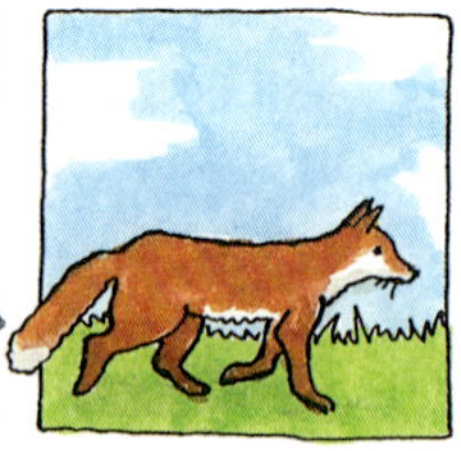
fox

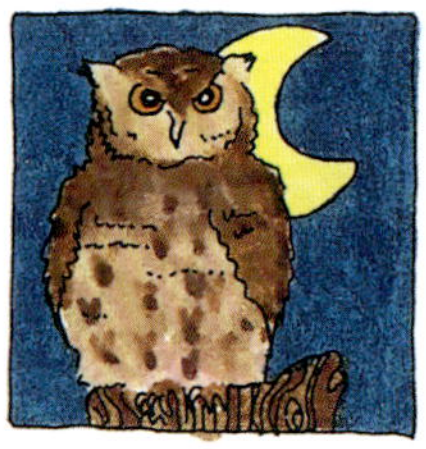
owl

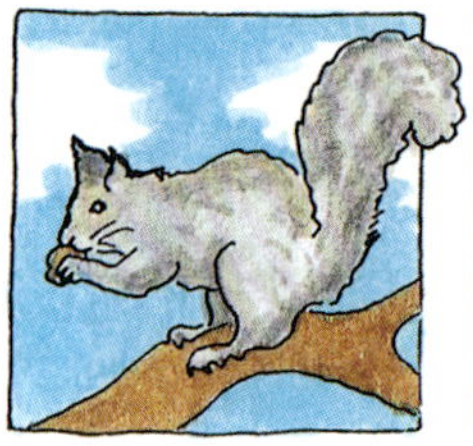
squirrel

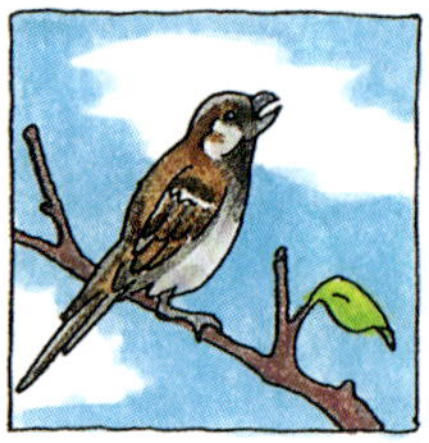
sparrow

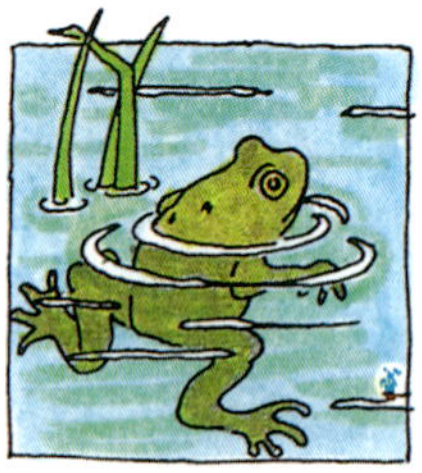
frog

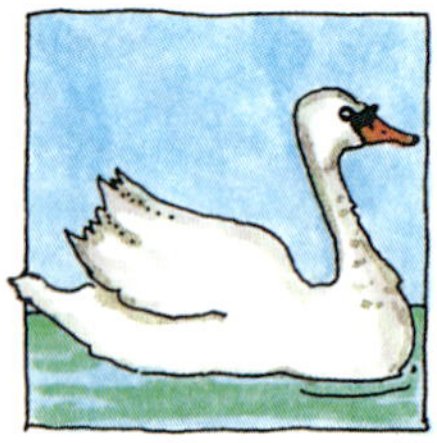
swan

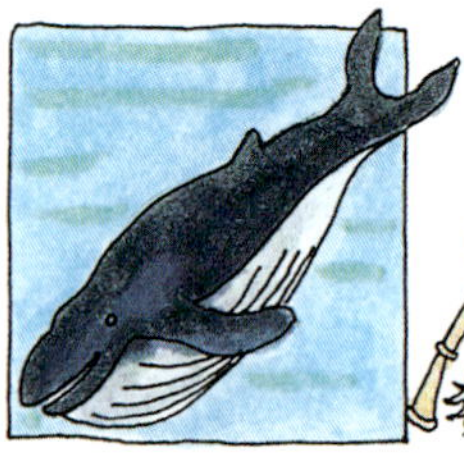
whale

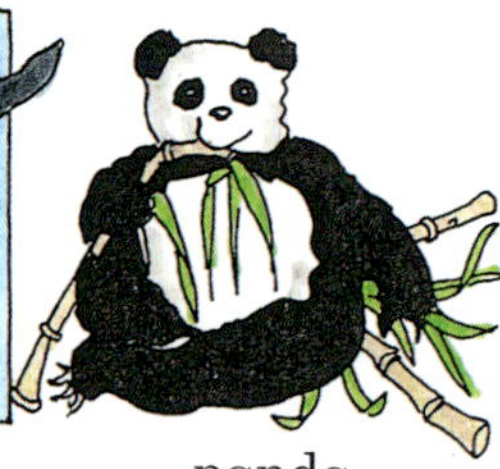
panda

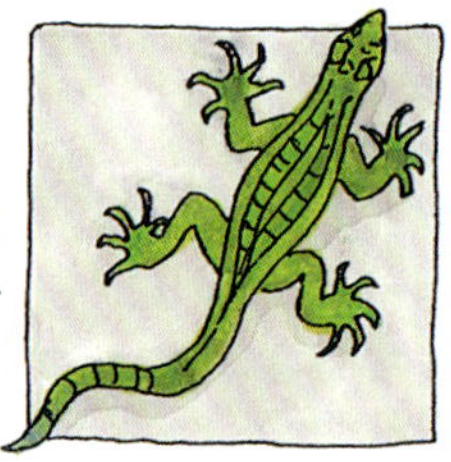
lizard

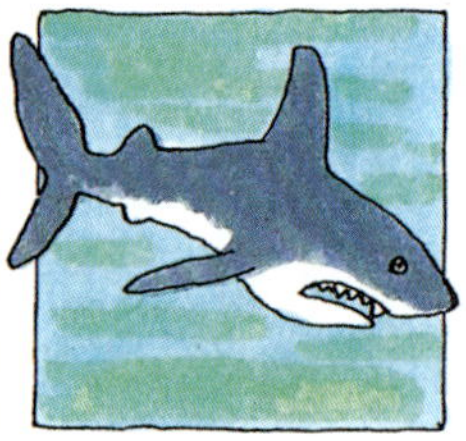
shark

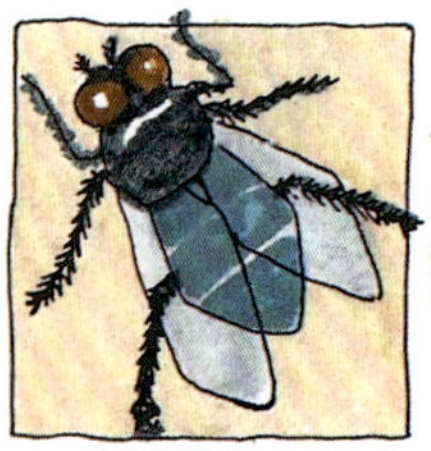
fly

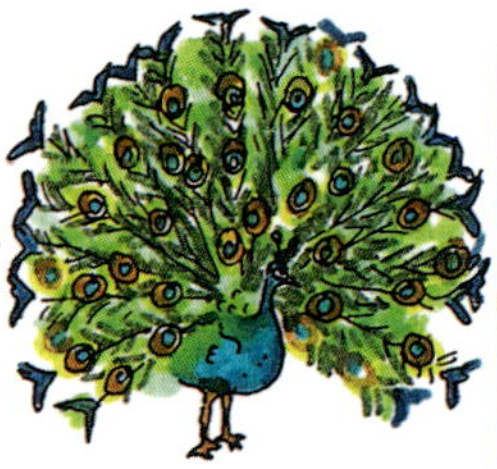
peacock

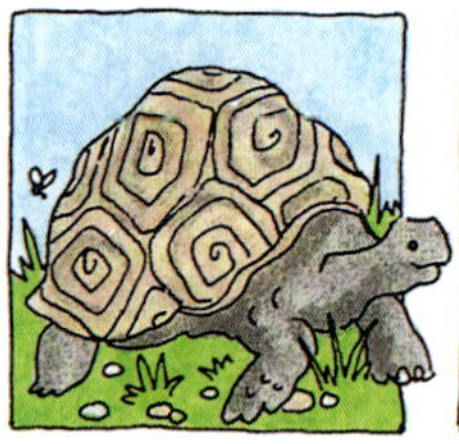
tortoise

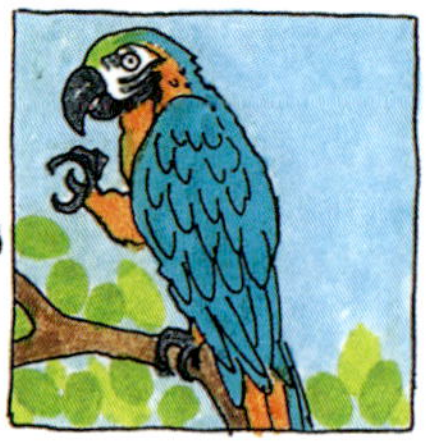
parrot

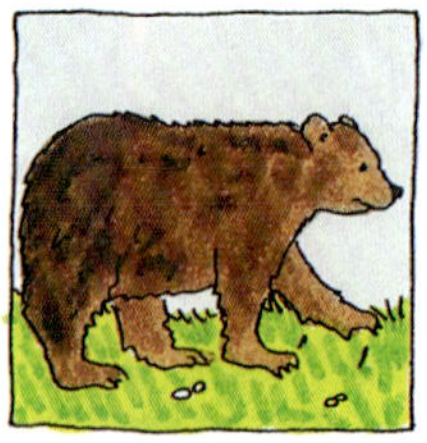
bear

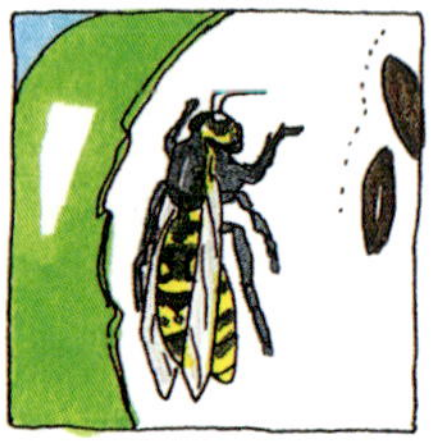
wasp

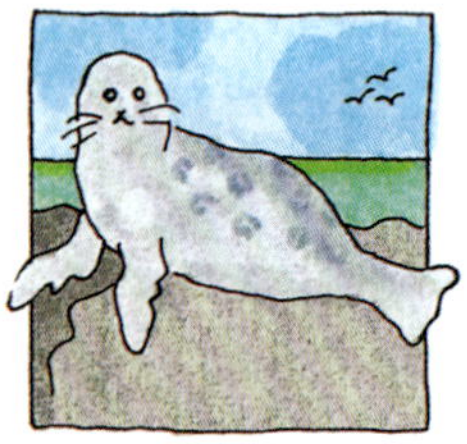
seal

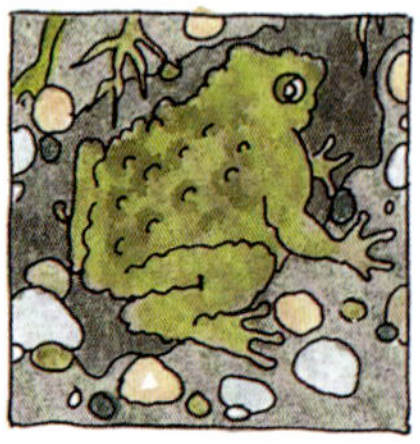
toad

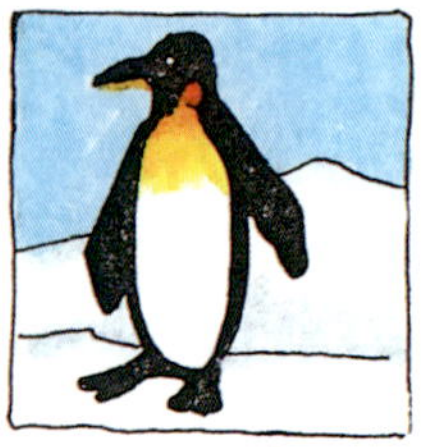
penguin

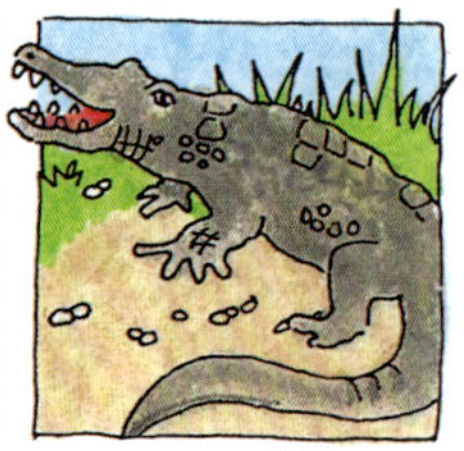
crocodile

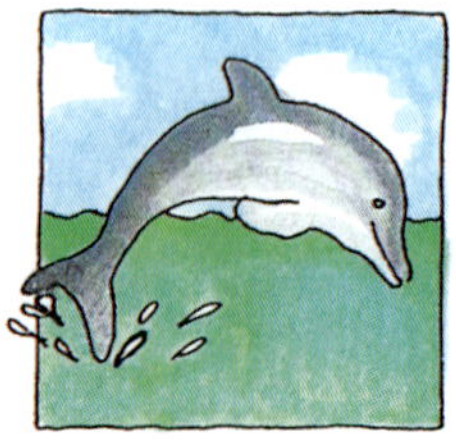
dolphin

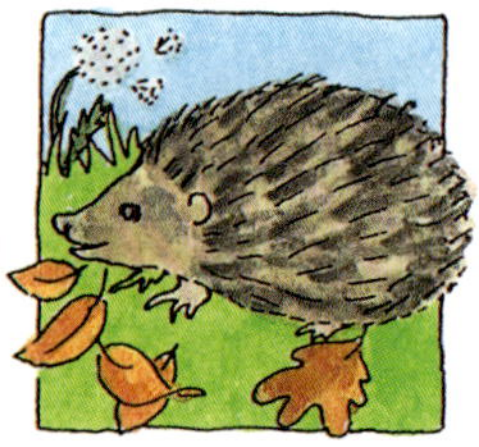
hedgehog

amphibian

reptile

mammal

bee

caterpillar

grasshopper

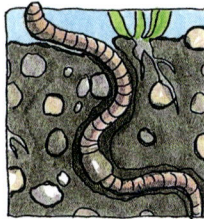
worm

ladybird

snake

turtle

ant

octopus

kangaroo   tail

butterfly

moth

snail

gerbil

mouse

puppy

budgerigar

beetle

hamster

kitten

pet

slug

goldfish

guinea pig

Mike and Jill have four pets, a dog,
two cats, and a rabbit.

How to use the wordlist

1 2 3 4 5 6 7 8 9

Numbers like this mean that there is a picture of the word.

| queen **47** 61 |

There is a picture of the word 'queen' on page 47.

1 2 3 4 5 6 7 8 9

Numbers like this mean that the word is in a story.

| queen 47 **61** |

The word 'queen' is in a story on page 61

On Saturday we went to Buckingham Palace. We saw the soldiers but we didn't see the Queen.

Aa

a (*each or for each*) 24 36
about (*a little before or after*) 11
about (*a little more or less than*) 36
about (*on the subject of*) 19 31 33
above 9 21
acrobat 34
across 21 64
act 35, acts, acting, acted
acting 35
actor 33
adventure 55
aerial 6 32
after 34 37 61
afternoon 11 33 61
again 29
airport 36 45
album 36
alien 56
alive 53
all (*every one of a group*) 34 37 43 49
all (*the whole of something*) 23 61
all right (*I agree*) 24
along 35 64
aluminium 29

am (*see be*) 25
ambulance 42
amphibian 70
angel 50
animal 67 69
ankle 3
another 9 29 41 57
answer 17 65, answers 69, answering, answered
answer 19
ant 70
antelope 68
any 24
anything 23 25 52
apple 24 27 65
apple juice 25
apple pie 26
are (*see be*)
aren't = are not
arm 3
armchair 5
armour 47
as (*like*) 29
as (*while*) 35
ask, asks 31 65 68 69, asking 31, asked
asleep 65
astronaut 33 **55**
at (*towards somebody or something*) 1 7 **14** 19 24 33 37 40 43 45 56 57 65 68

at (*a word that shows when*) 11 37 43 49 61
at (*a word that shows where*) 4 5 **9** 11 **14** 19 21 **25** 29 33 37 **40** 41 **43** 45 49 61 **67**
at the bottom 9 40
at the top 9
athletics 38
aubergine 23
audience 34
aunt 1 31 59 61
auntie (*aunt*) 1 14 40 45
autumn 52
axe 47

Bb

baby (babies) 1 4 40 45
back (*body*) **3**
back (*in or to the place where somebody or something was before*) 18 29 56 61
back (*the part that is behind the front*) 68
bacon 25
bad 4
badminton 38
bag 44 45
baked bean 26
baker 22
ball 16
ballet 12
balloon 28
banana 24
band 33
bandage 4
bang 49
bank 22
barbecue 27
bark, barks, barking 13, barked
barn 65
base 37
baseball 38
basketball 38
bat 38
bath 6 14
bathroom 6
battery (batteries) **32**
be (*a word that you use when you name or describe somebody or something*) 'This is Lucy.' 46, 'The sky is blue.' 51, 'Leo is on the stairs.' 5, 'It's twelve o'clock.' 11

be (*a word that you use with another verb*) 'What are you doing?' 'We're looking for Mum.' 21
be (*a word that you use with part of another verb to show that something happens to somebody or something*) 'Her teacher is called Miss Gwen.' 3, 'Uncle Paul is married to Sarah.' 1, 'newspapers are recycled' 29
be quiet 54
beach (beaches) **40** 59
beach umbrella 39
beak 69
bean 23 26
bear 69
beard 2
beautiful 53
because 5
bed 10 12 56
bedroom 6
bee 70
beetle 70
before 49
behind 9 65
bell 62
below 9
berry (berries) **52**
best 11 29 52 59 61 65
better than 51
between 9
bicycle 36 42
big 2 4 5 19 23 29 40 47 **53** 59 63 67
bike 36
bin 20 29
binoculars 40
bird 14 59 68 **69**
birthday 27
biscuit 26
bitter 54
black 2 47 52
black eye 4
blackboard 20
blast off 55, blasts off 55, blasting off, blasted off
blood 4
blossom 51
blow, blows 43, blowing, blew
blow up 49, blows up, blowing up, blew up
blue 2 5 40 51
blunt 54

board game 28
boarding card 45
boat 40 42 59 **62**
body (bodies) 3
boiled egg 25
bonfire 49
Bonfire Night 49
bonnet 41
book 15 19 34 36
bookcase 20
boot (*a shoe that covers your foot and ankle and sometimes part of your leg*) 2
boot (*car*) 41
born 59
both 55
bottle 30
bottom (*body*) 3
bottom (*the lowest part*) 9 40
bowl 8 27
boxing 37
box (boxes) **30** 36
boy 19
branch (branches) **65**
bread 25
break 12
breakfast 12
bridge 44 62 64
bring, brings, bringing 59, brought
British Isles 59
broken 4
broomstick 47
brother 1
brother's = brother is
brown 2 30 52 65
brown bread 25
bruise 4
brush, brushes 12, brushing, brushed
brush (brushes) 9
Brussels sprout 23
bucket 39
budgerigar 70
buffalo (buffalo *or* buffaloes) 68
build, builds, building, built 61
building 61
bull 66
bun 25 49
bunch (bunches) **23**
bus (buses) 12
bus stop 21
busby (busbies) **61**
bush (bushes) **52** 65
busy 13
butcher 21
butter 25
butterfly (butterflies) **70**

buy 43, buys 45,
buying 23, bought
by (*a word that shows
where*) 2 5 7 **9** 21 59
62 65 67
by (*'by car'*) **12**
by (*'divided by'*) **18**

Cc

cabbage 23
cabin 46
café 22
cake 8 27 50
calculator 10 19
calf (calves) **66**
call 1 49 61, calls,
calling, called 1 3 33
49 55 61 65
camcorder 31
came (*past of* **come**)
camel 68
camera 31
can (*be able to*) 2 10
17 29 34 37 40 41 46
52 59 68
can (*be allowed to*) 23
25 33 55 68 69
can 30
candle 27 49
canoe 38
canoeing 38
can't = can not
cap 30
capital city 60
car 12 14 21 32 **38** 41
45 47 68
car park 45
caravan 42
card (*greetings card*)
27 49 50
card (*playing card*) 36
41
card (*boarding card*)
45
cardboard box
(cardboard boxes) **30**
36
cardigan 2
carol 50
carpet 5
carrot 23
carry, carries,
carrying **15** 43,
carried
cartoon 33
cassette 27 32
cassette recorder 31
castle 47 59
cat 5 14 47 **70**
catch 11, catches **12**,
catching **16**, caught
caterpillar 70
cauldron 47

cauliflower 23
cave 40 47
CD 32
CD player 31
ceiling 20
celery 23
cereal 25
chain 41
chair 5 47
chalk 20
change 21, changes,
changing, changed
change 23
chase, chases, chasing
16, chased
cheap 54
check, checks 45,
checking, checked
cheek 3
check-in 45
cheese 26
cheetah 68
chemist 21
cherry (cherries) **24**
chess 11 35
chest 3
chest of drawers 9
chicken 26 66
child (children) 1 32
65
chimney 6
chin 3
chip 26
chocolate 26 49
choose, chooses 55,
choosing, chose
Christmas 50
Christmas carol 50
Christmas Eve 50
Christmas pudding
50
Christmas stocking
50
church (churches) 59
64
cinema 33
circle 19
circus (circuses) **34**
city (cities) 33 **60**
clap, claps, clapping
16, clapped
class (classes) 4 31 65
classical 33 35
classroom 20
claw 67
clean, cleans,
cleaning 2 **14**,
cleaned
clean 54
clear 30
cliff 40
climb, climbs,
climbing **16**, climbed
59

cloak 47
clock 8 9 62
closed 53
clothes 9 30 49
cloud 52
cloudy 52
clown 34
club 11 35 37
clue 34 63
coach (coaches) (*a bus
for taking people on
long journeys*) 42
coach (coaches) (*part
of a train*) **43**
coast 60
coat 2
cockpit 46
coconut 24
coffee 25
cola 25
cold (*illness*) 4
cold (*not hot*) 5 49 52
53
collar 57
collect 46, collects,
collecting 29,
collected
collecting stamps 36
colours 2
column 61
comb 9
come 14 65, comes 27
43, coming 21 43,
came 59, has come
57
come from 57 67,
comes from, coming
from, came from
come on 24
come out (*appear*) 49,
comes out, coming
out 40, came out
comedy show 34
compact disc 32
compasses 19
computer 10 31 36
55
computer game 56
computer room 20
concert 33
container ship 42
continent 57
control tower 46
cook, cooks, cooking
13 27, cooked
corner 21
cotton 35
couldn't = could not
(*past of* **can**) 59
counter 17
country (countries)
57 59 67
cousin 1 14 37 40 63
cow 66

cowboy 33
crash 55
cream 26
cricket 38
crisp 26 27
crocodile 69
croissant 25
cross 21, crosses,
crossing, crossed
cross (crosses) 49
crossing 22
crossroads 63
crossword 34
crown 47
crown jewels 62
cry, cries, crying **15**,
cried
cucumber 23
cup 8 25
cupboard 8
curly 53
curry (curries) **26**
curtain 5
cushion 5
customs 46
cut, cuts, cutting **13**,
cut
cut 4
cycling 36

Dd

dad (*father*) 1 5 7 14
25 27 34 36 37 40 49
daffodil 51
dance, dances,
dancing 27, danced
dancing 3 35
dark 54
day 11 33 36 49 51 65
dead 53
dear 27 59
decoration 50
deer (deer) **68**
dentist 29
departure lounge 45
desk 10 20
detective story
(detective stories) **34**
dice (dice) **17**
didn't = did not (*past
of* **do**)
different 37 47 56
difficult 54
dig, digs, digging **13**
67, dug
dining room 6
dinner 12
dinosaur 48 61
dirty 5 54
dishwasher 8 31
disk drive 32
dive 37, dives, diving,
dived

diving 38
divided by 18
do (*perform an action*)
14 34 37, does **12** 37,
doing 21 37 57, did
do (*a word that you
use with another
verb to make a
question*) 24 25 57,
does, did
do (*a word that you
use with another
verb when you are
saying 'not'*) 2 14 19
21 25 29 33 49 51 56
57 65, does 14 19 40
56 65, did 61
doctor 4
does (*see* **do**)
doesn't = does not
doing (*see* **do**)
dog 5 13 51 67 **70**
dolphin 69
donkey 65
don't = do not
door 5 9 14 47
down (*from the top
towards the bottom
of something*) 59 **64**
downstairs 14
dragon 48
drama 35
draw, draws 69,
drawing, drew
drawer 9
drawing 36
dress (dresses) 2 35
dressing gown 9
drink 25, drinks,
drinking 27, drank
drink 27
drive, drives, driving
65 67, drove
driver 44
dry 53
duck 66
dustbin 29
duty-free shop 45

Ee

each 23
eagle 69
ear 3
early 11
earth 55
east 60
Easter 49
Easter egg 49
easy 54
eat 27 49, eats, eating
27 52, ate
egg 25 49
eight (8)

eighteen (*18*)

eighty (*80*)

elbow 3

electric guitar 33

elephant 67

eleven (*11*)

else ('*anything else*') 23 25

empty 53

end 59 61

engine (*car engine, jet engine*) **41 46**

engine (*locomotive that pulls a train*) 43

entertainment 33

envelope 29

escalator 62

evening 11

every 36 37 51

everybody 14 27 40 45

everyone 25 50 57 59

everything 5 47 56

everywhere 47 50

except 5

excuse me 43

exercise book 19

expensive 54

eye 3

eyebrow 3

eyelash (eyelashes) 3

eyelid 3

Ff

face 3 49

fairy (fairies) **48**

fairyland 47

fall, falls, falling **16**, fell

fall off, falls off, falling off 2, fell off

fall over, falls over, falling over **16**, fell over

family (families) **1** 11 31 34 37 59

farm 65

farmer 65

fast 54

fat 53

father 1

Father Christmas 50

favourite 27 52 61

feather 68

feed, feeds, feeding 14 27 65, fed 61

feet (*plural of* **foot**)

fence 13

ferry (ferries) **42**

festival 49

field 63 65

fifteen (*15*)

fifty (*50*)

fight, fights, fighting **16**, fought

fight 27

fill, fills, filling 7, filled

filling station 41

film 33

find 10, finds, finding, found

finger 3

finish, finishes 11 18 56, finishing, finished

finish 18

fire 5

fire engine 42

fireplace 5

firework 49

first (*before doing anything else*) 31

first (*before all the others*) 34 41 63

fish (fish) **26 69**

fishing 35

fishing boat 42

fishing rod 35

five (*5*)

flag 57

flamingo 68

flat 21

flight 45

flipper 39

floor 20

floppy disk 32

flower 5 47 64

fly (flies) **69**

foal 65

fog 52

foggy 52

food 25 27

foot (feet) **3** 47 52 57

football 27 **38**

football team 38

footpath 63

for (*a word that shows the person or thing you are talking about*) 1 56

for (*a word that shows who will get or have something*) 4 29 35 40 45 50

for (*a word that shows where somebody or something is going*) 7

for (*a word that shows how something is used or why something is done*) 29 31 45 51

for (*with the meaning of*) 57

forehead 3

fork 8

forty (*40*)

fountain 62

four (*4*)

fourteen (*14*)

fox (foxes) **69**

freezer 8

fridge 8

friend 9 11 14 27 31 36 37 43 51

friendly 56 65

frighten 49, frightens, frightening, frightened

frightening 47 49

frog 69

from (*a word that shows where somebody lives or was born*) 57

from (*a word that shows when something starts*) 11

from (*a word that shows who gave or sent something*) 9 23 27

from (*a word that shows the place where you find something*) 7 27

from (*a word that shows what is used to make something*) 49

from (*a word that shows difference*) 56

fruit 23 24

fruit juice 25

frying pan 8

full 43 **53**

fun 35

funny (*strange*) 25

funny (*a person or thing that is funny makes you laugh or smile*) 65

fur 67

Gg

game 17 27 28 41 55 **69**

game show 34

garage 5

garden 5 14 27 32

gardening 35

garlic 23

gate 5 64

gave (*past of* **give**)

geese (*plural of* **goose**)

gerbil 70

get 41, gets 55, getting 7, got

get dressed, gets dressed **12**, getting dressed, got dressed

get into, gets into 55, getting into, got into

get up 11, gets up **12**, getting up, got up

ghost 49

giant 47

giraffe 68

girl 19 27 29

give 49 65, gives 29 45, giving 4 29 57, gave 49

glass (glasses) 8 25

glass (*the material*) 30

glasses (*spectacles*) **2**

globe 20

glove 2

glue 19

go (*move from one place to another*) 21 24 43 45 51 63, goes 29 45 47 55, going 9 34 41 43 45 47 56, went 21 59 61

go (*travel to a place to do something*) 11 35 37 56, goes **12** 37 51, going 40, went 36 59

goal 38

goat 65

goggles 39

going to 34

goldfish (goldfish) **70**

good 3 25 27 33 40

good at 37 55

Good Friday 49

goose (geese) **66**

gorilla 68

got (*see* **have got**)

grandad (*grandfather*) 1 59

grandfather 1

grandma (*grandmother*) 1 14 46 59

grandmother 1 45

grandpa (*grandfather*) 1 14 59

grandparent 1

granny (*grandmother*) 1 43 59

grape 24

grapefruit 24

grass (grass) **51**

grasshopper 70

great 34 36 59

great-granddaughter 46

green 2 30

grey 2 67

guard 44

guess 57 69, guesses, guessing, guessed

guide 33

guinea pig 70

guitar 33 36

gun 33

guy 49

Guy Fawkes 49

gym 20

gymnastics 12 37

Hh

had (*past of* **have**)

hair 3 12

hairdresser 21

half past 12

hall (*house*) **6**

hall (*school*) 20

Hallowe'en 49

hamburger 26 27

hammer, hammers, hammering **13**, hammered

hamster 70

hand 3

handlebar 41

hang-glider 38

hang-gliding 38

happy 25 27 33 50

hard 54

has (*see* **have**)

hat 2 57 61

hate 34 52, hates, hating, hated

have (*a word that you use with parts of other verbs to show that something happened or started in the past*) 4 56, has 57, having, had

have *also* have got (*own or keep*) 1 4 23 31 34 36 47 49 51 57 68 70, has *also* has got 1 4 19 27 47 51 63 65, had *also* had got

have *also* have got (*be ill with something*) 4, has *also* has got 4, had *also* had got

have (*used with many nouns to talk about doing something*) 11 24 25 36 49 67, has **12**, having 19 25 27 57, had 25

haven't = have not
having (see **have**)
hay 65
head 3
headache 4
headlight 41
headphones 32
hear, hears, hearing, heard 61
heart 49
heavy 53
hedge 13 65
hedgehog 69
heel 3
helicopter 46
helmet 36
help 23, helps, helping 7, helped
here you are (words that you say when you give something to somebody) 24
here's = here is
he's = he has ('He's come') 57
he's = he is
hide, hides, hiding **16**, hid
high 53
highest 59
hiking 35
hiking boot 35
hill 59 64
hip 3
hippo 68
hippopotamus (hippopotamuses or hippopotami) **68**
hit, hits 55, hitting **16**, hit
hobby (hobbies) **35**
hockey 37
hockey stick 37
hold, holds, holding 29, held
holiday 36
home 12 24 **32** 51 56
homework 12 31
honey 25
horn 67
horror film 33
horse 38 65
hospital 29
hot 5 49 52 **53** 61 65
hot cross bun 49
hot dog 27
hour 46
house 5 14 32 37 56 59 61
hovercraft 42
how many 27
how much 23
hundred (100)
hungry 19 25 65

hurry 43, hurries, hurrying, hurried
hurt, hurts, hurting, hurt 4, have hurt 4
hydrofoil 42

Ii

ice 52
ice cream 26 51
I'd = I would
I'll = I will
I'm = I am (see **be**)
in (wearing) 2 62
in (a word that shows where) 3 5 7 **9** 14 **15** 19 **21 23** 27 29 31 33 35 37 40 43 45 47 49 51 56 57 59 61 65 67
in (a word that shows when) 11 49 51 61
in (a word that shows how long) 18 43 46
in front of 10
in the middle 9 59
injection 4
insect 69
inside 62
into 14 29 45 47 55 **64**
iron, irons, ironing **13**, ironed
is (see **be**)
island 59
isn't = is not
it's = it is
I've = I have

Jj

jacket 2 65
jam 25
jar 30
jeans 2
jeep 42
jet engine 46
jigsaw puzzle 27
judo 37
jug 8
juggler 34
juice 25 27
jump, jumps, jumping **16**, jumped
just (only) 25

Kk

kangaroo 70
karate 37
ketchup 27
kettle 8
key 10
keyboard 32
kick, kicks, kicking **16**, kicked

kind (sort or type) 29
king 47
kiss 45, kisses 45, kissing, kissed
kit 27
kitchen 7 14
kite 28
kitten 70
kiwi fruit 24
knee 3
knee-pad 36
knife (knives) 8
knight 47
knitting 35
knitting needle 35
knock, knocks, knocking **14**, knocked
know 2 21 25 50 57, knows, knowing, knew

Ll

ladder 63
ladybird 70
lake 59
lamb 65
lamp 5 9
lamp-post 22
land 56, lands 46 56, landing 46, landed
land 59 67
landing 46
last 35
late 11
laugh, laughs, laughing **15**, laughed
launch pad 55
lawnmower 31
leaf (leaves) **52**
learn, learns, learning 31, learnt or learned
leave 68, leaves **12** 43, leaving, left
left 63
leg 3 68
leggings 2
lemon 24
lemonade 27
leopard 68
lesson 12 19 36
let's (you use 'let's' to ask somebody to do something with you) 24 25 34 51
letter 36
lettuce 23
library (libraries) **20**
lick, licks, licking 67, licked
lid 30

lie down, lies down, lying down **15**, lay down
lifeboat 42
light (something that makes light) **22 28** 32
light (not **heavy**) **53**
light (not **dark**) **54**
light bulb 32
lighthouse 40
lightning 52
like 14 19 24 25 33 35 37 40 51 59, likes 2 3 5 7 11 25 27 37 51 65 67, liking, liked 59 61
like (similar to) 67
liner 42
lion 61 **67**
lip 3
list 23
listen 35, listens, listening, listened
listening to music 35
litter bin 29
little 29 47 55
live 5 59, lives 21 61, living, lived
living room 6
lizard 69
London 9 36 43 49 **61**
Londoner 61
long 53 68
look (turn your eyes towards somebody or something) 21 24 34 45 51 57 65 68, looks 7 19 40 45 56, looking 1 **14** 33 37 40 43 65, looked 59
look (seem or appear) 56 67, looks 33 40 47 61, looking, looked
look for (try to find) 63, looks for 41, looking for 21, looked for
lorry (lorries) **42**
lose, loses 55, losing, lost
lot 37
lots 1 14 19 27 35 41 43 47 49 55 59 61
loudly 14
love 35 49, loves 37 40 50, loving, loved
love 59
lovely 46 49 61
low 53
luggage 45
lunch (lunches) **12** 19 25 61 63

lunch box (lunch boxes) 19
lunch break 11
lying down (see **lie down**) 15

Mm

machine 31 45
made (past of **make**)
magazine 29
magic 47
magic wand 47
magnet 30
make (to cause something to be or to happen), makes 5, making, made
make (to put things together so that you have a new thing) 49, makes, making 7 35 40, made 2 7 29
making models 36
mammal 70
man (men) 4 21 45 49
mane 67
many 27 29 59
map 19 58
margarine 25
market 21 23
marry, marries, marrying, married 1
mask 49
match 59, matches, matching, matched
maths 19
mean, means 49, meaning, meant
meat 25
medicine 3
melon 24
mend, mends, mending **13**, mended
merry (happy and full of fun) 50
microphone 32
midday 11
middle 9 59
midnight 11
milk 25
milk shake 25
mineral water 25
minus 18
minute 18 43
mirror 5
Miss (a word that you use before the name of a girl or woman who is not married) 3
moat 47
model 36

model kit 27
monkey 68
monster 48
month 51
moon 56
more 55
morning 11 33 35 61
moth 70
mother 1 4 21
motor boat 42
motor racing 38
motorbike 42
mountain 59
mouse (mice) 70
moustache 2
mouth 3 27
move, moves 17, moving, moved
Mr (*a word that you use before the name of a man*) 14 23 37 65
Mrs (*a word that you use before the name of a woman who is married*) 14 21 23
much 29 59
mug 8
mum (*mother*) 1 5 7 14 21 23 27 31 33 37 40 43 45 47 49 68
murder 33
museum 62
mushroom 23
music 33 35 56
music room 20
musical 33 35

Nn

name 1 49 57 62
narrow 53
nearly 7
neck 3
need 23, needs, needing, needed
needle 35
net 37
netball 11 37
new 27 34 36 54
new year 50
news 34
newsagent 21
newspaper 29 33
next 14 41
next to 9
night 11 49
nine (*9*)
nineteen (*19*)
ninety (*90*)
noise 5
noisy 37 53
north 60
nose 3 46

nothing 47
noticeboard 10
now (*at the present time*) 4 7 9 18 34 43 47 52 55
now (*because of what has happened*) 4 25 36 49
number 17 45 63
number plate 41
nurse 4
nut 24

Oo

o'clock 12 43
oar 35
octopus (octopuses) 70
off (*down or away from something*) 2 46 55
off (*at a distance from*) 59
often 35
Oh dear (*words that show you are surprised or unhappy*) 19 24 25
oil tanker 42
OK 25 34
old (*not young*) 53
old (*you use 'old' to show the age of somebody or something*) 19 65
old (*not new*) 29 36 49 54 59 61
on (*working*) 5
on (*a word that shows where*) 4 5 9 16 17 19 21 27 34 36 37 40 41 43 45 49 51 55 57 59 61 65 68
on (*a word that shows when*) 11 34 35 49 61
on (*a word that shows how you travel*) 59 61
on a treasure hunt 63
on holiday 36
one (*1*)
onion 23
only 24 33
onto 47
open, opens 47, opening, opened
open 5 53
opposite 53
orange (*colour*) 2
orange (*fruit*) 24
orange juice 27

orbit 55, orbits, orbiting 55, orbited
orchestra 33
ostrich (ostriches) 68
other 4 27 47 51 59 67
out (*away from a place*) 21 64
out of (*using*) 36 56
outside (*to a place not in a building*) 12
outside (*in a place that is close to a building*) 61
oven 8
over (*directly above something but not touching*) 5
over (*across to the other side of something*) 43 64
owl 69

Pp

paddle 38
paint, paints, painting 35, painted
paint 19
paintbrush 19
painting 29 35
palace 61
pancake 26
panda 69
pants 9
paper 20 29
parent 1 67
park, parks 45, parking, parked
park (*an open place in a town*) 36
park (*safari park*) 67
parrot 69
part 57
party (parties) 27 49 57
passenger 44
passport 45
passport control 45
past (*a word that shows how many minutes after the hour*) 12
past (*from one side of something to the other*) 21 68
path 13
patient 4
pavement 21
paw 67
pea 26
peach (peaches) 24
peacock 69
peanut 26
pear 24

pedal 41
pen 10 19
pence (*plural of penny*)
pencil 10 19
pencil case 19
pencil sharpener 19
penguin 69
penny (pence or pennies) 23
people (*plural of person*)
pepper ('*salt and pepper*') 8
pepper (*vegetable*) 23
perfume 45
person (people) 37 49 59
personal stereo 31
pet 70
petrol 41
petrol pump 41
photo 2 9 62
photograph 1
pick, picks, picking 51, picked
pick up (*take and lift something*), picks up, picking up 15 27, picked up
pick-up truck 42
picnic lunch (*picnic lunches*) 63
picture 19 33 36 49 59 62 69
pie 26
pig 65
pigeon 62
piglet 65
pill 4
pilot 46
pineapple 24
pink 2 68
pirate 48
pizza 27
plan 19
plane 36 46
planet 56
plant 9 29
plaster 3
plastic 29
plate 8
platform 44
play 35 37 41, plays 11 33 37 56, playing 17 27 40 41 55 65 69, played
play 33 35
playing cards 36
playing chess 35
playing on the computer 36
playing the guitar 36

player 41
playground 15
please 23 25
pleased 35
plug 32
plum 24
plus 18
point, points, pointing 59, pointed
point 41 55
police officer 21
pond 65
post office 22
postbox (postboxes) 22 64
postcard 10 59
postman (postmen) 59
poster 9
pot 29
potato (potatoes) 23 26
pound (*money*) 23
pound (*weight*) 24
pow 56
pram 22
present 28 49
printer 32
protractor 19
pudding 50
puddle 52
pull, pulls, pulling 13, pulled
pump 41
pumpkin 49
puppy (puppies) 70
purple 2 9
push, pushes, pushing 13, pushed
pushchair 22
put 4 17 49, puts 50, putting 7 9 29 40, put
put on (*take clothes and wear them*) 35, puts on 55, putting on, put on
pyjamas 10

Qq

quarter 12
queen 47 61
question 17 69
queue 43
quiet 53 56 59

Rr

rabbit 27 70
racing car 38
racket 38
radio 31

radish (radishes) **23**

rag 30

rain, rains, raining 51, rained

rain 51

rainbow 51

raspberry (raspberries) **24**

read 34 36, reads, reading 5 23, read

reading 36

really (*in fact*) 25 62

really (*very much*) 36

receipt 23

rectangle 19

recycle 29, recycles, recycling, recycled 29

recycling 29

recycling bin 29

red 2 21 49 52

reptile 70

restaurant 25

return 33, returns, returning, returned

rhinoceros (rhinoceros *or* rhinoceroses) **67**

rice 26

riding 38 59

right (*correct*) 2 57

right (*not left*) **64**

river 35 60 62

road 21 59 64

road sign 63

roast beef 26

rock 40

rock concert 33

rocket 55

roll 25

roller skate 36

roller skating 36

roof 6

room 9 13 20 47

rope 16

rose 35 49

rough 54

round 5 9 21 64

rounders 37

rowing 35

rowing boat 35

rubber 10 19

rubbish 29

rucksack 35 44

rug 5

rugby 38

ruler 10 19

run 52, runs 55, running **15** 40, ran

runner bean 23

runway 46

Ss

saddle 41

safari park 67

safe 56

sailing 36

Saint Valentine's Day 49

salad 26

salt 8

sand 39

sandal 2

sandcastle 39

sandwich (sandwiches) **27**

satellite 55

saucepan 8

saucer 8

sausage 27

save, saves, saving 29, saved

saw (*past of* **see**)

say 45 65, says 14 19 21 41 43 45 65 67, saying, said

scarf (scarfs *or* scarves) **2**

scary 40

school 9 11 19 29 37 59

science lab 20

scissors 19

score 41, scores 41, scoring, scored 56

screen 32

sea 40 56 59

seagull 40

seal 69

seaside 39

season 52

seat 44 45 63

seaweed 39

security 45

security officer 45

see (*know something using your eyes*) 2 21 33 40 41 45 52 59 61 68 69, sees 21 65, seeing, saw 21 59 61

see (*visit or meet somebody*) 4 43 45, sees, seeing, saw

see you soon 59

send 49, sends, sending, sent

seven (*7*)

seventeen (*17*)

seventy (*70*)

sew, sews, sewing 35, sewed

sewing 35

sewing machine 31

sh (*be quiet!*) *54*

shark 69

sharp 54

sheep (sheep) **65**

sheepdog 65

shelf (shelves) **19**

shell 39

she's = she is

shield 47

shine 56, shines, shining 51 56, shined

ship 40 42 47

shirt 2

shoe 2 9

shoot 56, shoots, shooting 56, shot

shop 21 30 45

shopping list 23

short 53

shorts 2

shoulder 3

shout, shouts 40, shouting **15** 40, shouted

show 45, shows, showing, showed

shower 12 67

shuttlecock 38

sightseeing 61

signpost 59

silver 48

silver paper 30

sing 35, sings 27, singing 5, sang

singing 11 35

sink 8

sister 1 43

sit 47, sits 68, sitting 5 9 **16** 21 40 52 65, sat

six (*6*)

sixteen (*16*)

sixty (*60*)

skateboard 36

skateboarding 36

skating (*ice-skating*) **12**

skating (*roller skating*) **36**

skeleton 49

ski 38

skiing 38

skip, skips, skipping **15**, shipped

skirt 2

sky (skies) **51** 56

sleep, sleeps, sleeping 67, slept

slipper 10

slow 54

slug 70

small 53 58

smile, smiles, smiling **15**, smiled

smooth 54

snail 70

snake 70

snorkel 39

snorkelling 40

snow, snows, snowing 51, snowed

snow 51

snowball 51

snowman (snowmen) **51**

sock 9

sofa 5

soft 54

soldier 61

some 4 7 15 24 25 27 29 37 40 41 45 49 51 61 64 65

someone 14 40

something 40

sometimes 35 37 49

son 4

soup 26

south 60

space 55

space shuttle 55

space station 56

spaceship 56

spacesuit 55

spade 39

spaghetti 26

sparrow 69

special 34

splash 47 56

spoke 41

spoon 8

sport 37

sports centre 37

sports field 20

spring 51

square (*on a board game*) **17**

square (*shape*) **19**

square (*open space in a town*) **61**

squash 38

squirrel 69

staffroom 20

stairs 5

stamp 36

stand, stands, standing **15** 21 43, stood

star 56

start, starts 11 43, starting, started

start 17

station 43 56 61

statue 61

stay 61, stays, staying 59, stayed 61

steak 26

steering wheel 41

stereo 27 31

steward 46

still 49

stomach 3

stop 21 41, stops, stopping, stopped

story (stories) **34**

straight 53

strawberry (strawberries) **24 51**

stream 63

streamer 28

strike 61, strikes, striking, struck

strong 53

sugar 25

suit 2

suitcase 44

summer 36 51

sun 40 51 55 56

sunbathe, sunbathes, sunbathing 40, sunbathed

sunbather 39

sunglasses 39

sunny 51

supermarket 22

swan 33 69

sweater 2 35

sweatshirt 2

sweep, sweeps, sweeping **13**, swept

sweet (*a small piece of boiled sugar*) **26**

sweet (*not bitter*) **54**

sweetcorn 26

swim 37 40, swims, swimming 40, swam

swimming 12 38

swimming pool 38

swimming trunks 39

swimsuit 39

swing, swings, swinging **16**, swung

switch (switches) **32**

sword 47

Tt

T-shirt 2 62

table 5 27 47

table tennis 37

tail 46 70

take (*go with somebody or something to another place*) 45, takes, taking 65, took

take (*put your hand round something and hold it*) takes 41 45, taking 43

take (*used with many nouns to talk about doing something*), takes, taking, took 2 61

take back (*return*) 29, takes back, taking back, took back

take off (*remove*), takes off, taking off 29, took off

take off (*leave the ground*), takes off, taking off 46, took off

take-off 46

talk, talks, talking 21, talked

tall 53

tap 8

taxi 62
tea 7 **25**
teacher 3 **20** 29 37 65
team 38
teapot 8
teatime 7
teddy bear 10
telephone 31
telephone box (telephone boxes) **22**
television 11 **31** 34 37
ten (10)
tennis 38
tennis court 38
textbook 19
thank you 4 23
thanks 25
that's = that is
theatre 33
there're = there are
there's = there is
they're = they are
they've = they have
thick 53
thin (not **fat**) 53
thin (not **thick**) 53
thing 29 61
think 2 43 49, thinks 65, thinking 19, thought
thirteen (13)
thirty (30)
three (3)
through 40 43 45 47 **64** 67
throw, throws 17, throwing **16**, threw
throw away 29
thumb 3
thunder 52
thunderstorm 52
ticket 43 45
ticket collector 44
ticket office 43
tidy, tidies, tidying **13**, tidied
tidy 53
tiger 67
tights 9
time 33 56
times 18
timetable 44
tin 29

tired 61
to (a word that shows where somebody or something is going) 1 **12** 17 21 27 29 34 35 37 41 43 45 47 49 55 57 59 61 **64** 65
to (a word that shows how many minutes before the hour) **12**
to (a word that shows when something finishes) 11
to (a word that shows how something changes) 21
to (a word that shows why) 4 29 41 43 45 67
to (a word that you use before verbs to make the infinitive) 1 14 27 34 37 40 43 52 56 61
toad 69
toadstool 52
toast 25
today 7 24 27 51 59
toe 3
toilet 6
tomato (tomatoes) **23** 25
tongue 3
too (more that you want or need) 2
too (also) 4 5 7 14 25 29 35 37 40 49 62 65 67 68
took (past of **take**)
tooth (teeth) 3
toothache 4
toothbrush (toothbrushes) **6**
toothpaste 6
top 9 50 60
tortoise 69
total 23
towards 64
towel 6
tower 46 62
town 21 59
toy 10 29
track 44
tractor 65
traffic lights 22
train 43 59

trainer 2
travel 41
treasure 48 63
treasure chest 48
treasure hunt 63
tree 27 **50** 51 56 63 65 67
triangle 19
tried (past of **try**)
trousers 2
trunk 67
try 37, tries 69, trying, tried 49
tub 29
tube 62
tunnel 44
turkey 50
turn 18
turn off 64, turns off, turning off, turned off
turn onto 64, turns onto, turning onto, turned onto
turtle 70
tusk 67
twelve (12)
twenty (20)
two (2)
tyre 41

Uu

ugh (the sound that you make when you think something is not nice) 54
ugly 53
umbrella 39 51
uncle 1 14 21 31 40 45 59
under 9 40 52 65
underground 62
untidy 53
until 11
up (into an upright position) 3
up (to a higher level or position) 59 **64**
upstairs 14
use 29, uses 29, using 67, used

Vv

vacuum cleaner 31
vampire 33

van 42
vase 5
vegetable 23 26
very 25 29 35 37 40 51 55 59 61
vest 9
video 12 32
video game 27
video recorder 31
violet 49
visit 55, visits, visiting 65, visited
volleyball 38

Ww

wait 45, waits, waiting 4 43 46, waited
walk 35 68, walks, walking **15**, walked 59
walk 51
wall (round a house) 5
wall (in a room) 9 **20**
wand 47
want 25 34 52, wants 40, wanting, wanted
wardrobe 9
warm 51
was (past of **be**) 35 36 59 61
wash 29, washes 29, washing 13, washed
wash up, washes up, washing up **13**, washed up
washbasin 6
washing machine 8 31
wasp 69
watch 34 37, watches **12**, watching 37 46, watched
watch (watches) **10**
water 5 7 14 **25** 27 47 67
water fight 27
water-skier 40
wave 45, waves 45, waving, waved
wave 40
way in 67

way out 68
weak 53
wear 49, wears, wearing 2 9 40 47 61, wore
week 11 36 37
weekday 11
weekend 37 61
we'll = we will
well 25 33
well done 56
went (past of **go**)
we're = we are
were (past of **be**) 61
west 60 61
western 33
wet 53
whale 69
what 5 19 25 34 37 46 52 68
what about? 25 33
what are you doing? 21 57
what's = what is
what's the matter? 4
wheel 41
wheelbarrow 13
when 35
where 9 21 46 57 59 63 65 67
which 55 57
whistle 44
white 2 5 30 63
white bread 25
who 2 41
why not? 68
wide 53
wildlife programme 34
will 4 23 25 34
win, wins 18 41, winning, won
wind 51
window 5 49 56 68
windscreen 41
windsurf, windsurfs, windsurfing 40, windsurfed
windsurfer 40
windy 51
wing 46 69
winter 52
wire 32
wish 50, wishes, wishing, wished
witch (witches) 47
with (having or carrying) 2 4 21 27 43 50 57 67

with (a word that shows people or things are together) 2 5 11 21 25 27 36 40 59 61
with (using) 2 7 40 45
with (against) 35
with (towards) 35
wizard 47
wolf (wolves) **67**
woman (women) 4 21
wood 63 67
wool 35
word 59
work, works, working 14 55, worked
work 14
world 57
worm 70
would like 25 34 37
wrestling 37
wrist 3
write 1 49, writes, writing 19, wrote
writing letters 36

Xx

X-ray machine 45

Yy

yacht 42
year 19 35 51
yellow 2 9 52
yesterday 25 59
yoghurt 26
young 53
you're = you are
you've = you have

Zz

zebra 68
zoom 55